APPLE iOS 18 REVIEW

(Plus Some Rumoured Features We Should Expect)

The Ultimate Guide to Apple's Most Advanced Update

Shirley Carls

Disclaimer:

The information in this article is based on rumours and speculations, not confirmed details from Apple.

Table of Contents

INTRODUCTION

When I think back to the early days of iOS, it feels like looking through a digital time capsule. The journey from the original iPhone's iOS to the monumental iOS 18 is nothing short of remarkable. Apple has continuously redefined the smartphone experience, and iOS 18 stands as the pinnacle of that evolution, bringing together years of innovation, feedback, and an unwavering commitment to user experience.

In the beginning, the iPhone revolutionised the way we interacted with our devices. The initial version of iOS, though groundbreaking, was relatively simple by today's standards. It introduced us to the concept of a touch-based interface, where tapping, swiping, and pinching became second nature. The App Store, launched with iOS 2, opened the floodgates for developers to create applications that would soon become integral parts of our lives.

As we moved from one version to the next, each iteration of iOS brought its own set of advancements and refinements. iOS 3 introduced copy and paste functionality, a seemingly small feature that had a big impact on usability. iOS 4 brought multitasking, allowing users to switch between apps seamlessly. With iOS 5, we saw the introduction of iCloud, syncing our data across devices and making it easier to keep everything in sync.

The leap to iOS 7 was perhaps one of the most significant changes in the history of Apple's operating system. It marked a complete visual overhaul, moving away from skeuomorphism towards a flat design language. This new aesthetic was cleaner, more modern, and laid the groundwork for the visual consistency we see in iOS today. It wasn't just about looks; iOS 7 also brought

Control Center, making essential settings more accessible, and revamped the Notification Center for better organisation.

From iOS 8 onwards, Apple focused heavily on enhancing functionality and integration. iOS 8 introduced HealthKit and HomeKit, setting the stage for the smart home and health tracking ecosystems. iOS 9 continued this trend, improving performance and battery life while adding features like Split View and Picture in Picture on the iPad, making it a more versatile device for both work and play.

With iOS 10, we saw the introduction of a more expressive Messages app, allowing users to send animated messages, stickers, and even handwritten notes. Siri became more powerful, integrating with third-party apps to perform a wider range of tasks. iOS 11 took these capabilities further, especially on the iPad, with a new Dock, improved multitasking, and the Files app, which brought a more desktop-like experience to the tablet.

iOS 12 focused on performance and stability, particularly for older devices. It also introduced Screen Time, giving users insights into their device usage and helping them manage their digital lives better. iOS 13 brought a system-wide Dark Mode, which quickly became a fan favourite, and significant updates to apps like Photos and Maps.

iOS 14 was a game-changer in terms of customization. Widgets on the Home Screen, the App Library, and Compact Calls all aimed to make the user experience more intuitive and personal. The privacy features introduced in iOS 14, such as App Tracking Transparency, underscored Apple's commitment to user privacy, giving users more control over their data.

Then came iOS 15, which focused on enhancing the ways we stay connected. FaceTime received a major update with spatial audio and SharePlay, allowing users to share experiences like watching movies or listening to music together during calls. The new Focus feature helped users minimise distractions by customising notifications based on what they were doing. Live Text brought the ability to interact with text in photos, making it easier to copy, paste, or look up information.

Now, with iOS 18, Apple has once again set the bar higher. This version of the operating system is poised to be the most significant upgrade in years, building on the foundation laid by its predecessors while introducing a slew of new features that push the boundaries of what's possible on a mobile device. At its core, iOS 18 is all about integrating artificial intelligence and generative AI across the system, making interactions more intelligent and personalised.

Siri, Apple's virtual assistant, has undergone a major transformation. Powered by advanced language models and AI, Siri is now more conversational and capable of handling complex queries and tasks. It can provide smarter, more personalised responses that take into account a user's context and history. Imagine asking Siri to plan your day, and it not only schedules your meetings but also suggests when you should take breaks based on your typical work patterns.

Beyond Siri, iOS 18 brings AI-powered features to other built-in apps and system functions. The Messages app can generate custom emoji and auto-complete sentences based on the content of your messages. Spotlight search has been enhanced with AI to surface more relevant information from across the operating system. Even the

Photos app benefits from AI, with new photo editing tools that make it easier to enhance and perfect your pictures.

The Home Screen experience is also more customizable than ever before. Users can place app icons anywhere on the grid, creating blank spaces and custom layouts to suit their preferences. The ability to change app icon colours adds another layer of personalization, allowing users to truly make their device their own.

As I reflect on the journey from iOS 7 to iOS 18, it's clear that Apple has never been content with standing still. Each version has built on the successes of the past, incorporating user feedback and leveraging new technologies to create a more powerful, intuitive, and enjoyable experience. iOS 18 is the culmination of years of innovation, a testament to Apple's vision and dedication to pushing the envelope.

In writing this book, I aim to take you through the intricate details of this evolution, exploring the technological advancements, design philosophies, and user-centric features that have defined each version of iOS. We'll delve into the specific enhancements in iOS 18, looking at how AI and generative technologies are transforming the way we interact with our devices. From the major overhaul of Siri to the customization options on the Home Screen, every feature has been thoughtfully designed to enhance our digital lives.

Join me on this journey as we explore the most upgraded version of iOS in Apple's history. Whether you're a longtime iPhone user or someone new to the ecosystem, there's something in iOS 18 that will enhance your experience and make you appreciate the innovation that goes into creating one of the world's most advanced operating systems.

Chapter 1: The Heart of iOS 18

Artificial Intelligence and Generative AI Integration

The dawn of iOS 18 marks a significant evolution in Apple's mobile operating system, with Artificial Intelligence (AI) and Generative AI integration taking centre stage. This chapter delves into the advancements in AI, its pivotal role in enhancing user experience, and the enhanced privacy and security features that make iOS 18 a game-changer.

Overview of AI Advancements

In recent years, AI has transitioned from a futuristic concept to a tangible reality, transforming the way we interact with technology. Apple has been at the forefront of this revolution, and with iOS 18, the company has taken significant strides in integrating advanced AI capabilities into its ecosystem.

AI in iOS 18 is not just about automating tasks; it's about making the operating system more intuitive, responsive, and personalised. One of the most notable advancements is the implementation of machine learning models that continuously learn and adapt to user behaviour. These models power a range of features, from predictive text input to personalised app suggestions, making the user experience seamless and efficient.

Generative AI, a subset of AI focused on creating new content, also plays a crucial role in iOS 18. This technology is behind some of the most innovative features in the new OS, such as the ability to generate custom emojis based on user inputs in the Messages app or creating personalised playlists in Apple Music. By leveraging generative AI, iOS 18 can provide users with content that is not only relevant but also uniquely tailored to their preferences.

Moreover, AI advancements in iOS 18 extend to image recognition and processing. The Photos app, for instance, uses AI to automatically categorise and tag photos, making it easier for users to find specific images. AI-powered photo editing tools offer enhancements and suggestions that previously required professional software, bringing advanced editing capabilities to the fingertips of everyday users.

The Role of AI in Enhancing User Experience

The integration of AI in iOS 18 is fundamentally about enhancing the user experience. Apple has always prioritized user-centric design, and AI takes this commitment to the next level by making the OS smarter and more responsive.

One of the standout features is the improved Siri, Apple's virtual assistant. Powered by advanced language models, Siri in iOS 18 is more conversational and capable of understanding complex queries. This transformation enables users to interact with their devices more naturally, reducing the friction typically associated with voice commands. For instance, users can now instruct Siri to perform multi-step tasks with a single command, such as taking a series of photos, creating a GIF, and sending it to a contact. This level of functionality significantly enhances the convenience and utility of Siri, making it an indispensable tool for many users.

AI also plays a crucial role in personalising the user experience. iOS 18's machine learning algorithms analyse user behaviour to provide more relevant app suggestions, notifications, and content. This personalization extends to the Home Screen, where users can place app icons anywhere on the grid, create custom layouts, and change app icon colours. By understanding user preferences and habits, iOS 18 ensures that the device feels uniquely tailored to each individual.

Another area where AI shines is in predictive text and autocorrect features. The keyboard in iOS 18 uses AI to predict the next word or phrase a user might type, significantly speeding up text input. This predictive capability is also context-aware, meaning it takes into account the conversation's context to provide more accurate suggestions. This results in a more fluid and less error-prone typing experience.

Furthermore, AI enhances the functionality of built-in apps. The Messages app, for example, can auto-complete sentences and generate custom emojis based on the conversation's content. The Photos app's AI-powered editing tools offer users suggestions to improve their photos, such as adjusting brightness or cropping, making high-quality photo editing accessible to everyone.

Enhanced Privacy and Security Features

With the integration of AI, privacy and security have become even more critical. Apple has always championed user privacy, and iOS 18 is no exception. The new OS includes several enhanced privacy and security features designed to protect user data and maintain trust.

One of the key privacy features in iOS 18 is on-device processing. Unlike other virtual assistants that rely on cloud processing, Siri performs most of its operations directly on the device. This approach ensures that user data does not leave the device, providing an additional layer of privacy and security. By processing data locally, Apple minimises the risk of data breaches and unauthorised access.

AI in iOS 18 also helps in detecting and mitigating security threats. The OS uses machine learning to identify suspicious activities and potential security breaches. For example, the system can detect unusual login attempts or unauthorised access to sensitive information and take appropriate action to protect the user. This proactive approach to security ensures that users are always one step ahead of potential threats.

Moreover, iOS 18 introduces enhanced privacy controls, giving users more transparency and control over their data. The new privacy dashboard provides a comprehensive overview of how apps are using personal data, allowing users to make informed decisions about their privacy settings. Users can see which apps have accessed their location, microphone, camera, and other sensitive data, and revoke permissions if necessary.

Apple has also implemented stricter app review guidelines to ensure that all apps in the App Store adhere to high privacy standards. Apps must clearly explain how they collect and use data, and they are required to seek explicit user consent before accessing sensitive information. This commitment to privacy extends to third-party apps, ensuring that the entire iOS ecosystem upholds Apple's privacy principles.

In conclusion, the heart of iOS 18 lies in its advanced AI and generative AI integration, which significantly enhance the user experience while maintaining robust privacy and security features. The AI advancements make the OS smarter, more responsive, and personalised, transforming how users interact with their devices. By prioritising on-device processing and providing enhanced privacy controls, Apple ensures that users can enjoy the benefits of AI without compromising their privacy. iOS 18 sets a new standard for mobile operating systems, blending cutting-edge technology with a steadfast commitment to user-centric design and privacy.

Chapter 2: Siri's Major Overhaul

Siri's Transformation: Advanced Language Models and AI

Siri's transformation in iOS 18 marks a significant leap forward, primarily driven by the integration of advanced language models and artificial intelligence (AI). This overhaul is designed to make Siri not only smarter but also more intuitive and capable of understanding and responding to users in a manner that feels almost human.

The incorporation of advanced language models is at the heart of this transformation. These models, built on the latest advancements in natural language processing (NLP) and machine learning, allow Siri to comprehend and generate human-like text based on the input it receives. These models can parse complex sentences, understand context, and generate responses that are not only accurate but also contextually relevant.

One of the most significant improvements is Siri's ability to understand nuances in human speech. Traditional voice assistants often struggled with understanding variations in accents, slang, and colloquial language. However, with the new language models, Siri can now process and understand a broader range of linguistic inputs. This capability is particularly beneficial in a diverse user base where accents and dialects vary widely.

Additionally, the advanced AI integrated into Siri allows it to learn and adapt over time. This learning is not limited to understanding language better but also extends to understanding individual user preferences. By analyzing user interactions, Siri can provide more personalized responses and suggestions, making the user experience more tailored and efficient. For instance, if a user frequently asks about certain topics or uses specific phrases, Siri can adapt to these preferences and provide quicker, more accurate responses in future interactions.

Moreover, the use of advanced AI and language models means that Siri can now handle more complex linguistic structures and ambiguities. For example, understanding a sentence like "Can you book me a table for two at the nearest Italian restaurant tonight?" requires not just voice recognition but also the ability to understand context (booking a table), the subject (an Italian restaurant), the number of people (two), and the time frame (tonight). Siri's new capabilities allow it to parse and act on such complex requests more accurately and swiftly than ever before.

Enhanced Conversational Capabilities

One of the most exciting aspects of Siri's overhaul in iOS 18 is its enhanced conversational capabilities. These improvements make interactions with Siri feel more natural and fluid, bridging the gap between human and machine communication.

The new conversational model enables Siri to maintain context over multiple interactions, allowing for more dynamic and engaging dialogues. Previously, Siri's responses were often limited to single, isolated queries. Now, with the ability to remember the context of a conversation, Siri can follow up on previous queries, ask clarifying questions, and provide more detailed and helpful responses.

For instance, if a user starts a conversation by asking, "What's the weather like today?"

and follows up with "What about tomorrow?" Siri can understand that the user is still inquiring about the weather and provide the relevant information without needing the user to specify the context again. This continuity in conversation makes interactions smoother and more intuitive.

Additionally, Siri's improved conversational abilities include better handling of interruptions and corrections. In real-life conversations, it's common for people to change their minds or correct themselves mid-sentence. Siri can now handle these changes gracefully, making it easier to adjust commands or queries without starting over. For example, if a user says, "Set a reminder for 5 PM," and then corrects to "Actually, make it 6 PM," Siri can seamlessly update the reminder without requiring the entire command to be reissued.

Another significant enhancement is the incorporation of more natural speech patterns and tones. Siri's responses are now crafted to sound less robotic and more conversational, incorporating natural pauses, intonations, and even expressions of empathy or humor when appropriate. This change not only makes interactions more pleasant but also helps build a more personable and engaging user experience.

Furthermore, the enhanced conversational capabilities extend to handling more casual and social interactions. Siri can now participate in small talk, provide jokes, or engage in light-hearted banter, making it more than just a functional assistant but also a companion in daily life. This development opens up new possibilities for how users interact with their devices, transforming Siri from a tool into a more relatable and enjoyable presence.

Handling Complex Queries and Tasks

One of the standout features of Siri's overhaul in iOS 18 is its improved ability to handle complex queries and tasks. This advancement makes Siri a far more powerful and versatile tool for users, capable of assisting with a wide range of activities that previously required multiple steps or manual intervention.

The new Siri can process multi-step commands seamlessly. For example, a user can now ask Siri to perform a series of tasks in one go, such as "Send a message to John saying I'm running late, then play my workout playlist, and set a reminder to call the vet at 3 PM." Previously, such a request would have required multiple interactions. Now, Siri can execute these commands in a single, fluid sequence, significantly enhancing user productivity and convenience.

In addition to multi-step commands, Siri's ability to integrate and interact with third-party apps has been significantly improved. This means that users can now control and interact with a broader range of applications through Siri, extending its functionality beyond Apple's ecosystem. For instance, users can ask Siri to book a ride through a third-party ride-hailing app, order food, or even control smart home devices from various manufacturers, all through voice commands.

Moreover, Siri's enhanced capabilities include better handling of ambiguous or incomplete queries. When faced with a query that lacks sufficient detail, Siri can now ask follow-up questions to clarify the user's intent and gather the necessary information to complete the task. For example, if a user says, "Book a table for dinner," Siri might respond with, "Sure, for how many people and at what time?" This interactive process ensures that Siri can provide more accurate and useful assistance.

Another key improvement is Siri's ability to manage and execute more sophisticated tasks, such as scheduling meetings across different time zones, creating detailed itineraries, or generating complex reminders and to-do lists. For instance, users can ask Siri to "Create a travel itinerary for my trip to New York," and Siri can compile a detailed schedule, including flight information, hotel reservations, and suggested activities, all based on user preferences and past interactions.

Siri's enhanced task management capabilities are further bolstered by its improved integration with Apple's ecosystem of apps and services. This integration allows Siri to access and utilize data from apps like Calendar, Reminders, Mail, and Notes more effectively. For example, users can ask Siri to "Find an available meeting slot this week with Mark," and Siri can cross-reference the user's calendar with Mark's availability (if shared) and suggest suitable times.

In summary, the overhaul of Siri in iOS 18 represents a significant step forward in making Apple's virtual assistant more intelligent, intuitive, and capable. The integration of advanced language models and AI, enhanced conversational capabilities, and the ability to handle complex queries and tasks make Siri a more powerful and indispensable tool in users' daily lives. This transformation not only enhances the user experience but also sets the stage for even more sophisticated interactions and capabilities in future updates.

Chapter 3: AI-Powered Features Across the System

Messages App:Custom Emoji Generation

The Messages app in iOS 18 takes personalization to the next level with its custom emoji generation feature. Imagine sending an emoji that not only reflects your mood but is also uniquely crafted based on the content of your conversation. This groundbreaking feature uses advanced AI algorithms to analyse your text and generate emojis that are contextually relevant and expressive.

For instance, if you're chatting about a recent hiking trip, the app might generate an emoji of a person hiking, complete with a backpack and a scenic backdrop. This level of detail and customization makes your messages more engaging and fun. The AI behind this feature considers various factors such as the keywords in your text, the tone of the conversation, and even your past interactions to create emojis that truly resonate with your message.

The custom emoji generation is not just about fun; it also enhances communication. Emojis are a powerful tool for conveying emotions and nuances that might be lost in plain text. By offering personalised emojis, the Messages app ensures that your messages are more expressive and meaningful. This feature is particularly beneficial in group chats where conveying the right emotion quickly is crucial.

Auto-Complete Sentences

Another revolutionary feature in the Messages app is the AI-powered auto-complete sentences. Gone are the days of typing out long messages manually. With iOS 18, the Messages app intelligently predicts and completes your sentences, making texting faster and more efficient.

The auto-complete feature leverages deep learning models trained on vast amounts of text data. This enables the app to understand the context of your conversation and predict the most likely next words or phrases. For example, if you start typing "I'm thinking about going to...", the app might suggest "the beach this weekend. Want to join?". This prediction is based on common patterns in language usage and the context of your current and previous conversations.

What sets this feature apart is its ability to learn and adapt to your personal writing style over time. The more you use it, the better it becomes at predicting what you want to say. This not only speeds up your typing but also ensures that your messages sound like you. The app's AI is designed to respect privacy, performing all processing on-device without sending your data to the cloud, thus maintaining your confidentiality and security.

Spotlight Search

AI-Enhanced Information Surfacing

Spotlight Search in iOS 18 is smarter and more intuitive than ever, thanks to the integration of advanced AI. The enhanced information surfacing capability means that finding what you need on your device is quicker and more accurate.

Spotlight Search uses machine learning algorithms to understand your search habits and preferences. When you type a query, the AI analyses not just the keywords but also the context and your previous searches to deliver the most relevant results. For example, if you frequently search for documents related to a project you're working on, Spotlight will prioritise those documents in your search results.

This contextual understanding extends to how Spotlight handles information from across your device. It can pull relevant data from apps, emails, messages, and even the web, presenting it in a coherent and organised manner. If you search for "meeting notes," Spotlight might show you recent emails, calendar events, and documents related to your meetings, all in one place.

The AI enhancements also mean that Spotlight can now offer proactive suggestions. If it detects that you regularly check the weather or your calendar in the morning, it will surface this information without you even having to search for it. This level of personalization makes using your device more seamless and intuitive.

Photos App

AI-Powered Photo Editing Tools

The Photos app in iOS 18 is set to revolutionise how we edit and manage our pictures with its AI-powered photo editing tools. These tools bring professional-grade photo editing capabilities to the average user, making it easier to enhance and perfect your photos with just a few taps.

At the core of these new features is advanced machine learning that can analyse the content of your photos and suggest appropriate edits. For instance, the AI can detect faces, landscapes, and objects in your photos and provide editing options tailored to each type. If you have a photo with poor lighting, the app might suggest adjustments to brightness, contrast, and saturation to improve the overall look.

One of the standout features is the automatic enhancement tool. With a single tap, the AI can apply a series of edits to optimise your photo. This includes adjusting exposure, correcting colours, and even removing unwanted objects from the background. The results are impressive, often rivalling those achieved with more complex photo editing software.

Additionally, the Photos app includes AI-powered filters and effects. These are not your average filters; they are designed to complement the content of your photo. For example, a sunset photo might get a filter that enhances the warm tones and adds a subtle vignette to highlight the sun. The AI ensures that the filters enhance rather than overpower the natural beauty of your photos.

Another exciting feature is the ability to create personalised photo albums and slideshows. The AI can group photos based on events, locations, and even the people in them. It can then create a dynamic slideshow complete with music and transitions, turning your photos into a memorable video that you can share with friends and family.

In summary, the AI-powered features in the Photos app make photo editing accessible to everyone. Whether you're a seasoned photographer or someone who just wants to improve their vacation snaps, these tools provide a powerful and user-friendly way to enhance your photos. The integration of AI ensures that the editing process is not only quick and easy but also produces stunning results that you'll be proud to share.

The AI-powered features across the Messages app, Spotlight Search, and Photos app in iOS 18 exemplify Apple's commitment to leveraging cutting-edge technology to enhance user experience. These features not only make your device more intuitive and responsive but also add a layer of personalization and efficiency that was previously unattainable. Whether you're communicating, searching for information, or editing photos, iOS 18 ensures that your interactions are smarter, faster, and more enjoyable.

Chapter 4

Customizable Home Screen Experience

Personalization and Flexibility: Placing App Icons Anywhere

One of the most anticipated features in iOS 18 is the newfound flexibility in placing app icons anywhere on the Home Screen. Gone are the days when users were restricted by the rigid grid system that forced app icons to align in a specific order. With iOS 18, Apple has listened to the demands of its users, offering a more dynamic and personalised Home Screen experience.

Imagine being able to arrange your Home Screen in a way that truly reflects your personality and workflow. Want your most-used apps clustered together in a bottom corner for easy access with one hand? No problem. Prefer to have a minimalist approach with just a few essential apps on the screen? You can do that too. This level of customization allows users to tailor their Home Screen layout to their specific needs, enhancing usability and personal satisfaction.

This new feature is particularly beneficial for those who have a large number of apps but only use a select few regularly. By strategically placing these frequently used apps in accessible locations, users can streamline their interaction with their device. For example, a user might place their messaging apps in a cluster on the right side of the screen for quick access, while relegating less-used apps to the outer edges or secondary pages.

Creating Blank Spaces and Custom Layouts

In addition to the freedom of placing app icons anywhere, iOS 18 introduces the ability to create blank spaces on the Home Screen. This might sound trivial, but it marks a significant shift in how users can design their interface. Blank spaces can be used to separate groups of apps, creating a more organised and visually appealing layout.

Imagine having a Home Screen that isn't cluttered with app icons, but rather, thoughtfully spaced out. For instance, a user could have a row of productivity apps at the top, a blank space in the middle, and a row of entertainment apps at the bottom. This separation not only makes it easier to find apps but also reduces visual clutter, making the screen look more organised and less overwhelming.

Creating custom layouts with blank spaces can also be a form of self-expression. Users can design their Home Screen to reflect their personal style, whether that's a clean and minimalist look or a more eclectic and dynamic arrangement. This feature is particularly appealing to those who enjoy aesthetic customization, as it allows for a high degree of creativity in how the Home Screen is presented.

Moreover, this flexibility can improve accessibility for users with disabilities. For example, creating larger gaps between icons can make it easier for individuals with motor impairments to accurately tap on the desired app without accidentally selecting another one. It's a thoughtful inclusion that underscores Apple's commitment to making their devices more inclusive and user-friendly.

Changing App Icon Colours

Another exciting addition in iOS 18 is the ability to change the colours of app icons. This feature opens up a new world of personalization, allowing users to customise the appearance of their apps to match their preferred aesthetic or mood. Whether you want a cohesive colour scheme or a vibrant rainbow of icons, the choice is yours.

Changing app icon colours can significantly enhance the visual appeal of the Home Screen. Users can match their app icons to their wallpaper, creating a harmonious and stylish look. For instance, if your wallpaper features a beach scene, you might choose to change your app icons to shades of blue and sandy beige to complement the background.

This feature is not just about aesthetics; it can also improve usability. For example, users can colour-code their apps based on function. Productivity apps could be one colour, social media apps another, and entertainment apps yet another. This visual categorization makes it easier to locate and access specific types of apps quickly, reducing the time spent searching through multiple pages or folders.

Furthermore, the ability to change app icon colours can be particularly useful for users with visual impairments. High-contrast colour schemes can make it easier for these users to distinguish between different apps, improving overall accessibility. It's a small change that can have a significant impact on the user experience for individuals with various needs.

A New Era of Home Screen Customization

The introduction of these customizable features in iOS 18 represents a significant shift in Apple's approach to the Home Screen. For years, iOS users have been asking for more flexibility and personalization options, and with this update, Apple has delivered. These changes are not just about making the Home Screen look good; they're about creating a more user-centric and adaptable interface.

The ability to place app icons anywhere, create blank spaces, and change app icon colours allows users to craft a Home Screen that works for them. It's a move towards a more personalised and flexible iOS experience, where users have greater control over how their device looks and functions.

This level of customization can enhance productivity by allowing users to design their Home Screen in a way that aligns with their workflow. For instance, professionals can create a Home Screen layout that prioritises work-related apps, while keeping personal apps out of sight but within easy reach. Students can organise their apps by class or subject, making it easier to access the tools they need for studying.

In essence, iOS 18 empowers users to make their device truly their own. It acknowledges that every user is different, with unique preferences and needs. By offering these customization options, Apple is not only enhancing the aesthetic appeal of the Home Screen but also improving its functionality and accessibility.

As we continue to integrate technology into our daily lives, the importance of a personalised and user-friendly interface cannot be overstated. iOS 18's customizable Home Screen features are a step in the right direction, providing users with the tools they need to create a digital environment that suits their individual lifestyles. It's an exciting time for iOS users, as they explore the endless possibilities of their new, more flexible Home Screen.

Chapter 5: Rumoured Features and Enhancements

Apple Maps: Custom Routes and Topographic Maps

Apple Maps has always been a core part of iOS, helping millions navigate their daily lives, explore new places, and discover hidden gems. With iOS 18, Apple Maps is set to receive some of its most significant updates yet, making it not only a tool for navigation but a companion for adventurers and explorers.

Custom Routes

One of the standout features in the rumoured updates is the ability to create custom routes. Imagine planning a road trip where you want to visit specific landmarks, take scenic detours, and stop at your favourite eateries along the way. Custom routes in Apple Maps will allow you to do just that. This feature empowers users to plan their journeys with unparalleled flexibility. You can select multiple destinations, specify the order of stops, and even choose preferred routes based on your criteria—whether it's the fastest, the most scenic, or the most direct path.

This customization is perfect for cyclists, hikers, and drivers who want to avoid highways or toll roads. By integrating real-time traffic updates and weather conditions, Apple Maps can suggest optimal routes that adapt to changing circumstances, ensuring that you always have the best travel experience. This level of detail turns Apple Maps into a more personal travel guide, catering to individual preferences and needs.

Topographic Maps

For the outdoor enthusiasts, iOS 18 promises topographic maps within Apple Maps. These maps will display detailed information about the terrain, including elevation changes, trails, and natural landmarks. This is a game-changer for hikers, mountain bikers, and outdoor adventurers who rely on accurate topographical data to plan their trips.

Topographic maps will highlight trails with difficulty ratings, estimated times, and points of interest along the way. For those planning an adventure in the wilderness, this feature is invaluable. You can see the elevation profile of your hike, identify potential water sources, and find the best spots for breathtaking views. By incorporating these detailed maps, Apple Maps becomes a versatile tool for both urban navigation and wilderness exploration.

Apple Music: Auto-Generated Playlists and Smarter Transitions

Apple Music has always been at the forefront of delivering a seamless music experience, and the iOS 18 update aims to take it a notch higher with intelligent features that cater to your listening habits and preferences.

Auto-Generated Playlists

Imagine opening Apple Music and finding a playlist curated just for you, based on your recent listening history, mood, and even the time of day. The auto-generated playlists feature in iOS 18 promises exactly that. Using advanced algorithms and AI, Apple Music will analyse your listening patterns to create playlists that match your current vibe. Whether you're in the mood for some upbeat tunes for a workout, calming music for relaxation, or a mix of genres for a road trip, Apple Music will have you covered.

These playlists will update regularly, introducing you to new artists and songs that align with your tastes. It's like having a personal DJ who knows exactly what you want to hear next. This feature not only enhances your listening experience but also helps you discover new music effortlessly.

Smarter Transitions

Another exciting rumoured feature is smarter transitions between songs. No more abrupt changes that disrupt the flow of your listening experience. Apple Music will use AI to blend tracks seamlessly, ensuring smooth transitions that maintain the mood of your playlist. This technology analyses the beats per minute (BPM), key, and energy levels of songs to create transitions that feel natural and cohesive.

For instance, when moving from an upbeat pop song to a mellow acoustic track, Apple

Music will gradually adjust the tempo and volume, making the transition feel like part of a live DJ set. This attention to detail transforms your playlists into curated experiences that keep you engaged from start to finish.

Apple News: AI-Generated Summaries

In today's fast-paced world, staying updated with the latest news can be a challenge. With iOS 18, Apple News aims to make this easier and more efficient with AI-generated summaries.

Quick Overviews with AI-Generated Summaries

Imagine having a busy day and only a few minutes to catch up on the news. The AI-generated summaries feature will provide concise overviews of news articles, allowing you to get the gist of a story in seconds. Using natural language processing and machine learning, Apple News will extract the key points from articles and present them in a clear and readable format.

This feature is particularly useful for professionals, students, and anyone with a tight schedule who needs to stay informed without spending hours reading full articles. By offering these summaries, Apple News ensures that you can quickly grasp the essential details and stay updated with the world's events.

These summaries will also be customizable, allowing you to choose topics that interest you the most. Whether it's technology, politics, sports, or entertainment, Apple News will prioritise summaries in your preferred categories, making your news feed more relevant and personalised.

Calculator App: Sidebar for Recent Calculations and Improved Unit Conversion Interface

The Calculator app in iOS has long been a staple for quick maths calculations. With iOS 18, it's set to become even more functional and user-friendly.

Sidebar for Recent Calculations

One of the most anticipated features is the introduction of a sidebar that displays your recent calculations. This is a handy addition for anyone who needs to refer back to previous calculations without re-entering data. Whether you're balancing your budget, working on a project, or performing complex mathematical operations, the sidebar will help you keep track of your work.

You can scroll through your recent calculations, edit them, and even save important results for future reference. This feature enhances productivity by reducing the need to re-enter data and allowing you to focus on your tasks.

Improved Unit Conversion Interface

The unit conversion interface is also set to receive an upgrade. The new design will make it easier to switch between different units of measurement, whether you're converting currency, weight, length, or temperature. The interface will be more intuitive, with clear categories and quick access to common conversions.

By integrating the unit conversion tool more seamlessly into the Calculator app, iOS 18 makes it a one-stop solution for all your calculation needs. This enhancement is particularly useful for travellers, students, and professionals who frequently work with different units of measurement.

Calendar and Reminders Integration: Simplified Task and Event Management

Managing your time and staying organised is crucial, and iOS 18 aims to make this easier with deeper integration between the Calendar and Reminders apps.

Unified Task and Event Management

The new integration will allow you to manage your tasks and events from a single interface. You can create reminders directly within the Calendar app, set due dates, and receive notifications, ensuring that you never miss an important task or appointment. This unified approach simplifies time management, making it easier to plan your day and stay on top of your commitments.

For example, if you have a meeting scheduled in your calendar, you can add related tasks as reminders, such as preparing documents or sending follow-up emails. This integration ensures that all your tasks and events are interconnected, providing a comprehensive view of your schedule.

CarPlay Enhancements: Accessibility and Voice Recognition Improvements

CarPlay is an essential feature for many iOS users, providing a safer and more convenient way to use your iPhone while driving. With iOS 18, CarPlay is set to become even more accessible and user-friendly.

Enhanced Accessibility Features

One of the key enhancements is improved accessibility features for CarPlay. These updates aim to make CarPlay more usable for individuals with disabilities, including better support for voice commands and screen readers. By enhancing accessibility, Apple ensures that CarPlay is inclusive and beneficial for all users.

Improved Voice Recognition

Voice recognition is another area that will see significant improvements. With advanced AI and machine learning, CarPlay will understand voice commands more accurately, allowing you to control your apps and functions without taking your hands off the wheel. This enhancement makes driving safer and more convenient, as you can easily navigate, send messages, and control music using natural language commands.

Control Center Redesign: Updated Music Widget and Improved HomeKit Controls

The Control Center is a vital part of iOS, providing quick access to essential functions and settings. In iOS 18, it's getting a fresh redesign to improve usability and functionality.

Updated Music Widget

The music widget in the Control Center will receive an update, offering more controls and a better user interface. You'll be able to see album artwork, skip tracks, and adjust volume more easily. This enhancement makes controlling your music simpler and more intuitive, allowing you to enjoy your tunes without navigating through multiple screens.

Improved HomeKit Controls

HomeKit controls are also set to improve, making it easier to manage your smart home devices from the Control Center. The new interface will provide quicker access to frequently used devices and scenes, allowing you to control your home environment with just a few taps. Whether you're adjusting the thermostat, turning off lights, or checking security cameras, the improved HomeKit controls streamline the process, enhancing your smart home experience.

The rumoured features and enhancements in iOS 18 promise to make it one of the most exciting updates yet. From AI-powered improvements and enhanced customization to better integration and accessibility, iOS 18 is set to elevate the user experience to new heights. As we look forward to these innovations, it's clear that Apple continues to push the boundaries of what's possible, ensuring that iOS remains at the forefront of mobile operating systems.

Chapter 6: Fitness and Health App Innovations

Fitness App Overhaul: New Features and Improved User Experience

The iOS 18 release marks a significant overhaul of the Fitness app, positioning it as a comprehensive health and wellness hub for users. This transformation is driven by a suite of new features designed to enhance user experience, personalization, and engagement.

One of the standout additions is the Activity Rings 2.0. This updated version of the popular feature now includes more granular metrics, allowing users to track not just their movement, exercise, and standing hours, but also specific activity types like stretching, strength training, and mindfulness exercises. These new metrics are visually represented through dynamic, customizable rings that adapt to individual fitness goals and preferences.

Incorporating Adaptive Workouts is another groundbreaking feature. Leveraging AI, the Fitness app now analyses users' past workout data to suggest personalised exercise routines that match their fitness levels, goals, and even their mood. For instance, if the app detects a user has had a stressful day based on heart rate variability data, it might suggest a calming yoga session instead of a high-intensity workout.

The Social Fitness feature is designed to foster community and motivation. Users can join virtual workout groups, participate in challenges with friends and family, and share their progress on social media platforms. This social integration aims to create a supportive environment where users can encourage each other, celebrate milestones, and stay motivated.

To further enhance the user experience, the app now includes Real-Time Coaching. Users can receive instant feedback on their form and performance through voice and visual cues during workouts. This feature uses advanced motion sensors and AI to analyse movements and provide suggestions for improvement, helping users avoid injuries and maximise the effectiveness of their exercises.

Additionally, the Workout of the Day (WOD) feature curates daily workouts based on user preferences and fitness goals. This dynamic feature ensures variety and keeps workouts fresh, preventing the monotony that often leads to workout fatigue.

The Integration with Apple Watch has also been improved. Now, the Fitness app can sync more seamlessly with the watch, providing real-time updates and personalised feedback right on the wrist. This deep integration allows for features like heart rate monitoring, step counting, and even blood oxygen level tracking, all in one place.

Finally, the app's interface has undergone a Complete Redesign to make navigation more intuitive. The new design prioritises ease of use, with a clean, minimalistic look that emphasises important data and reduces clutter. Users can now access their workout history, performance stats, and goals with just a few taps, making it easier than ever to stay on top of their fitness journey.

The overhaul of the Fitness app in iOS 18 reflects Apple's commitment to helping users lead healthier, more active lives. With these innovative features and improved user experience, the app stands out as a versatile tool for fitness enthusiasts and beginners alike.

Health App

Mental Health Tracking

In an era where mental well-being is increasingly recognized as vital to overall health, iOS 18 introduces Mental Health Tracking in the Health app. This feature is designed to help users monitor and manage their mental health through a combination of self-reporting tools, sensor data, and AI-driven insights.

Users can now log their moods, stress levels, and emotional states throughout the day. The app provides prompts to encourage regular check-ins, making it easier to track patterns and identify triggers. This data is then analysed to offer personalised suggestions for improving mental health, such as mindfulness exercises, breathing techniques, or changes in routine.

The Health app also integrates with wearable devices to monitor physiological indicators of stress, such as heart rate variability and sleep quality. By combining this data with user inputs, the app can provide a comprehensive picture of one's mental health and offer tailored recommendations.

Furthermore, the app includes resources for mental health education, offering articles, videos, and exercises designed to help users develop healthier habits and coping strategies. This holistic approach aims to empower users to take proactive steps in managing their mental well-being.

Sleep Analysis

Understanding the importance of restorative sleep, iOS 18 enhances the Health app Sleep Analysis capabilities. This feature now provides deeper insights into sleep patterns, helping users improve their sleep quality and overall health.

The app tracks various sleep metrics, including total sleep time, sleep stages (light, deep, and REM), and sleep consistency. It uses data from the Apple Watch and other connected devices to provide a detailed analysis of sleep patterns and offer personalised recommendations for improvement.

One of the standout features is the Smart Sleep Scheduler, which helps users set and maintain a consistent sleep schedule. The app uses AI to analyse sleep patterns and suggest optimal bedtimes and wake-up times based on individual needs and lifestyle.

Additionally, the app provides Sleep Hygiene Tips, offering guidance on how to create a conducive sleep environment, such as maintaining a cool, dark bedroom, reducing screen time before bed, and establishing a relaxing pre-sleep routine. These recommendations are tailored to the user's specific sleep data, making them more effective.

The integration of Wind Down and Wake Up features further enhance the sleep experience. Users can set routines that include calming activities like reading, listening to music, or practising mindfulness before bed. In the morning, the app offers gentle wake-up alarms that sync with the user's sleep cycle to ensure a smoother transition from sleep to wakefulness.

Third-Party Fitness App Integration

To provide a more comprehensive health and fitness experience, the Health app in iOS 18 offers enhanced Third-Party Fitness App Integration. This feature allows users to sync data from various fitness and health apps into the Health app, creating a unified platform for tracking and managing their health.

Users can import data from popular fitness apps like Strava, MyFitnessPal, and Fitbit, among others. This integration ensures that all health metrics, from workouts to nutrition, are available in one place, providing a holistic view of the user's health and fitness journey.

The app also supports integration with specialised health apps, such as those for managing chronic conditions or tracking specific health metrics like glucose levels or menstrual cycles. By consolidating this data, the Health app can offer more accurate and personalised insights and recommendations.

New Workout Modes

The introduction of New Workout Modes in the Health app caters to diverse fitness preferences and goals. These new modes include activities like HIIT (High-Intensity Interval Training), Pilates, Tai Chi, and more, expanding the app's versatility and appeal.

Each workout mode comes with tailored metrics and tracking capabilities. For instance, the HIIT mode monitors heart rate zones and calorie burn more accurately, while the Pilates mode focuses on flexibility and core strength metrics. These specialised tracking features help users get the most out of their workouts.

The app also includes Adaptive Workout Plans that adjust based on user performance and progress. These plans are designed to evolve with the user, providing appropriate challenges and ensuring continuous improvement.

Redesigned Fitness+ Interface

Finally, the Health app's integration with Fitness+ has been significantly enhanced with a Redesigned Interface. The new design offers a more immersive and engaging user experience, with improved navigation and access to a wider range of workout classes and programs.

The interface features personalised recommendations based on user preferences, workout history, and fitness goals. Users can easily discover new classes, join live sessions, and track their progress in real-time. The integration also supports multi-user profiles, making it easier for families to share the Fitness+ experience while maintaining individual data privacy.

Additionally, the redesigned interface includes Interactive Elements such as real-time metrics displayed on-screen during workouts. These metrics provide immediate feedback, helping users stay motivated and on track with their fitness goals.

With these innovations, the Fitness and Health apps in iOS 18 offer a powerful combination of features designed to promote holistic health and wellness. Whether tracking mental health, improving sleep, integrating third-party apps, exploring new workout modes, or enjoying an enhanced Fitness+ experience, users have the tools they need to lead healthier, more active lives.

Chapter 7: Productivity and Accessibility Features

Freeform App: "Scenes" Feature for Easier Navigation

The Freeform app, a standout addition in iOS 18, promises to revolutionise how users interact with large and complex boards. This app is designed to enhance creativity and productivity, making it easier to brainstorm, collaborate, and organise thoughts. Central to this transformation is the innovative "Scenes" feature.

Imagine navigating a vast, intricate board filled with ideas, notes, and visual elements. Traditionally, finding specific sections within such an expansive space can be challenging. The "Scenes" feature addresses this by allowing users to create distinct segments or "scenes" within a board. Each scene acts as a focused area, making it easier to manage and navigate large projects.

Switching between scenes is seamless, thanks to intuitive keyboard shortcuts and a new user interface (UI) that streamlines the process. Whether you're a student organising study materials, a professional managing multiple projects, or a creative mind mapping out a story, the "Scenes" feature ensures you can move fluidly between different sections of your board.

Furthermore, scenes can be shared individually, enabling more targeted collaboration. Team members can focus on specific aspects of a project without being overwhelmed by the entire board. This feature not only boosts productivity but also enhances the collaborative experience, making the Freeform app an indispensable tool in the digital workspace.

Keynote and Pages AI Boost: Automatic Slide and Text Generation

The integration of artificial intelligence (AI) into Keynote and Pages marks a significant leap forward for Apple's productivity suite. This AI boost is designed to enhance efficiency and creativity, allowing users to generate content quickly and effectively.

In Keynote, AI-driven automatic slide generation takes the hassle out of creating professional presentations. By analysing the content you input, the AI can suggest slide layouts, incorporate relevant images, and even generate slide transitions. This feature is particularly beneficial for busy professionals who need to prepare presentations swiftly without compromising on quality.

Pages, on the other hand, benefits from AI-powered text generation. Whether you're drafting a report, writing a story, or composing an email, the AI can assist by suggesting relevant content, improving grammar, and ensuring coherence. This not only saves time but also helps in maintaining a high standard of writing.

The AI boost in Keynote and Pages extends beyond simple suggestions. It learns from your writing style and preferences, making increasingly accurate and personalised recommendations over time. This dynamic adaptability ensures that the tools grow with you, becoming more effective and intuitive the more you use them.

Moreover, these AI enhancements are designed to be user-friendly. You don't need to be a tech expert to harness their full potential. The integration is seamless, working in the background to enhance your productivity without disrupting your workflow.

Magnifier App Enhancements: New Reader Mode

The Magnifier app has long been a vital tool for users with visual impairments, allowing them to zoom in on text and objects for better clarity. With iOS 18, the Magnifier app receives a significant upgrade in the form of a new Reader mode, further enhancing its functionality and accessibility.

Reader mode transforms how users interact with text on their screens. By simplifying and magnifying text, this feature ensures that reading digital content becomes less strenuous and more enjoyable. It strips away unnecessary elements like ads and pop-ups, presenting a clean and focused reading experience.

This enhancement is particularly beneficial for individuals with dyslexia or other reading difficulties. Reader mode adjusts text size, spacing, and font to optimise readability, making it easier to comprehend and retain information. Additionally, it supports text-to-speech functionality, allowing users to listen to content if they prefer.

The new Reader mode in the Magnifier app exemplifies Apple's commitment to accessibility. It ensures that all users, regardless of their visual capabilities, can access and enjoy digital content with ease. By integrating these features into the operating system, Apple continues to lead the way in creating inclusive technology that caters to a diverse user base.

Mail App: Suggested Replies to Emails

Managing emails can be a daunting task, especially for those who receive a high volume of messages daily. The Mail app in iOS 18 addresses this challenge with the introduction of suggested replies, a feature designed to streamline email communication and enhance productivity.

Suggested replies leverage AI to analyse the content of incoming emails and propose appropriate responses. This can be particularly useful for handling routine queries and confirmations. For instance, if you receive an email requesting a meeting, the Mail app might suggest replies such as "Yes, that works for me," "Can we reschedule?" or "Please send more details."

This feature not only saves time but also ensures that responses are timely and relevant. It reduces the cognitive load of drafting replies, allowing users to focus on more critical tasks. Additionally, suggested replies can be customised to match your tone and style, making them feel more personal and less automated.

The integration of suggested replies in the Mail app is part of a broader effort to enhance user efficiency and communication. By automating routine tasks, this feature allows users to manage their inbox more effectively, ensuring that important emails are addressed promptly and professionally.

Messages App Innovations: RCS Support, Per-Word Effects, Custom Emojis

The Messages app in iOS 18 introduces a suite of innovations that elevate the messaging experience to new heights. These enhancements include Rich Communication Services (RCS) support, per-word effects, and custom emojis, each designed to make communication more engaging and expressive.

RCS Support

RCS support brings a new level of functionality to the Messages app. It allows for more advanced messaging features such as text effects, higher-quality media sharing, and read receipts. This upgrade transforms the app into a more robust and versatile communication tool, comparable to popular messaging platforms like WhatsApp and Facebook Messenger.

Per-Word Effects

Per-word effects add a creative dimension to text messaging. Users can now apply animations and visual effects to individual words within a message, making their communications more dynamic and expressive. Whether you're celebrating a friend's achievement or adding emphasis to a point, per-word effects provide a fun and engaging way to enhance your messages.

Custom Emojis

The ability to generate custom emojis based on the content of your messages is another standout feature. Using AI, the Messages app can create unique emojis that reflect the mood and context of your conversation. This not only makes messaging more personalised but also adds a layer of creativity and fun to everyday communications.

Annotations Features: Built-In Recording Tool and Transcription, Mathematical Notation Support

The introduction of advanced annotation features in iOS 18 represents a significant enhancement in how users can interact with and annotate their documents and notes. These features include a built-in recording tool with transcription capabilities and support for mathematical notation, catering to a wide range of professional and academic needs.

Built-In Recording Tool and Transcription

The built-in recording tool allows users to record audio notes directly within the app. This is particularly useful for students, journalists, and professionals who need to capture spoken information quickly. What sets this feature apart is its real-time transcription capability. As you record, the app transcribes the audio into text, providing an instant and accurate record of the conversation.

This dual functionality simplifies the process of taking and organising notes. Users can refer back to the original audio if needed, while the transcription provides a searchable text record. This ensures that important information is easily accessible and reduces the likelihood of missing critical details.

Mathematical Notation Support

For users in academic and scientific fields, the inclusion of mathematical notation support is a game-changer. This feature allows users to insert and display complex equations and symbols within their annotations. Whether you're a student solving equations or a researcher documenting findings, this capability ensures that your notes are comprehensive and precise.

The mathematical notation support integrates seamlessly with other annotation tools, allowing users to combine text, audio, and equations in a single document. This enhances the versatility and functionality of the app, making it a powerful tool for a wide range of users.

In summary, the productivity and accessibility features in iOS 18 reflect Apple's commitment to enhancing the user experience through innovative technology. From the Freeform app's "Scenes" feature to AI-boosted tools in Keynote and Pages, these enhancements are designed to streamline workflows, improve accessibility, and foster creativity. Whether you're managing emails, navigating large projects, or engaging in dynamic messaging, iOS 18 provides the tools you need to work smarter and more efficiently.

Chapter 8: Enhanced Notifications and Photo Features

AI-Generated Notifications: Managing and Prioritising Messages

With iOS 18, Apple has taken a significant leap forward in the realm of notifications, leveraging the power of artificial intelligence (AI) to create a more intuitive and efficient system for managing and prioritising messages. Gone are the days when users had to sift through a barrage of notifications to find what truly mattered. Instead, iOS 18 brings a smarter, more personalised approach to how notifications are delivered and organised.

Personalised Notification Management

At the core of this upgrade is the use of advanced AI algorithms that learn from user behaviour over time. iOS 18's notification system analyses which types of notifications a user interacts with most frequently and which ones are often dismissed. By understanding these patterns, the system can automatically prioritise the notifications that are most relevant to the user.

For instance, if you regularly engage with notifications from a particular messaging app but tend to ignore updates from a news app, iOS 18 will adjust accordingly. Critical messages from your preferred contacts will be highlighted and brought to the forefront, while less important updates are quietly relegated to the background. This personalised approach ensures that you never miss important communications while reducing the clutter from less pertinent alerts.

Contextual Relevance

One of the standout features of AI-generated notifications in iOS 18 is their contextual relevance. The system doesn't just prioritise notifications based on past behaviour; it also takes into account the current context. For example, if you have a meeting scheduled on your calendar, iOS 18 will ensure that notifications related to that event are given priority. Similarly, if you're driving, the system will minimise distractions by only allowing critical notifications to come through, enhancing both convenience and safety.

Smart Summaries

Another innovative feature is the introduction of smart summaries. Instead of bombarding users with individual notifications, iOS 18 groups related notifications into concise summaries. These summaries are intelligently categorised, making it easy to glance at your screen and get a quick overview of what's new. For instance, you might see a summary of social media updates, another for work-related emails, and a third for personal messages. This organisation not only saves time but also reduces the cognitive load of processing multiple alerts.

AI-Powered Do Not Disturb

The enhanced Do Not Disturb mode in iOS 18 also benefits from AI integration. The system can now predict when you might not want to be disturbed based on your routine and habits. For example, if you typically have a workout session every morning, iOS 18 will automatically activate Do Not Disturb during that time, ensuring you stay focused and uninterrupted. Additionally, you can customise the settings to allow only specific types of notifications to break through, such as urgent calls from family members.

Real-Time Adaptation

What truly sets iOS 18's notification system apart is its ability to adapt in real-time. The AI continuously learns and evolves, making adjustments based on new patterns and preferences. If you start using a new app frequently, iOS 18 will quickly recognize this change and adjust the notification priority accordingly. This dynamic adaptation ensures that the system remains responsive to your evolving needs and habits.

Photo App: AI-Powered Photo Retouching

The Photo app in iOS 18 has undergone a remarkable transformation, with AI-powered photo retouching tools that make it easier than ever to enhance and edit your photos. Whether you're a professional photographer or a casual user, these new features offer powerful capabilities that were once reserved for complex photo editing software.

Intelligent Photo Enhancement

At the heart of the Photo app's new capabilities is intelligent photo enhancement. With a single tap, users can now apply sophisticated adjustments that automatically improve the quality of their photos. The AI analyses various aspects of the image, such as lighting, colour balance, and composition, and makes precise adjustments to enhance the overall appearance. This feature is perfect for users who want to quickly enhance their photos without delving into detailed editing.

Advanced Retouching Tools

For those who prefer more control over their edits, iOS 18 introduces a suite of advanced retouching tools powered by AI. These tools include features such as blemish removal, skin smoothing, and object removal. What sets these tools apart is their ability to understand the context of the photo. For example, the blemish removal tool can accurately identify and remove imperfections on a subject's face without affecting the surrounding details. Similarly, the object removal tool can seamlessly erase unwanted elements from the background, maintaining the natural look of the photo.

AI-Powered Filters and Effects

iOS 18 also brings a new range of AI-powered filters and effects that allow users to get creative with their photos. These filters are not just simple overlays; they are designed to analyse the content of the photo and apply enhancements that complement the existing elements. For instance, a landscape photo might receive a filter that enhances the sky's colour while preserving the natural look of the trees and water. Users can preview these effects in real-time, making it easy to find the perfect look for their photos.

Seamless Integration with iCloud

One of the key advantages of the new Photo app is its seamless integration with iCloud. All edits and enhancements are automatically synced across your devices, ensuring that you always have access to the latest versions of your photos. This integration also enables collaborative editing, allowing you to share photos with friends and family who can then add their own edits and enhancements. The AI-powered tools ensure that these collaborative edits are applied seamlessly, maintaining a consistent look and feel across all devices.

Personalised Suggestions

To make the photo editing process even more intuitive, iOS 18 includes personalised suggestions within the Photo app. Based on your editing history and preferences, the app can recommend specific enhancements and filters for your photos. These suggestions appear in a dedicated section, allowing you to quickly apply them with a single tap. This feature not only saves time but also helps users discover new ways to enhance their photos.

Enhanced Privacy and Security

Apple has also prioritised privacy and security in the new Photo app. All AI-powered enhancements are processed directly on the device, ensuring that your photos remain private and secure. Unlike cloud-based photo editing services, iOS 18's Photo app does not require you to upload your photos to external servers. This on-device processing guarantees that your personal moments stay protected while benefiting from the power of AI.

User-Friendly Interface

The Photo app's interface has been redesigned to accommodate these new features while maintaining ease of use. The intuitive layout allows users to access all editing tools with minimal effort, making the photo enhancement process enjoyable and straightforward. Whether you're applying a quick enhancement or diving into detailed retouching, the streamlined interface ensures a smooth and efficient workflow.

With iOS 18, Apple has revolutionised the way users manage notifications and edit photos. The AI-generated notifications provide a smarter, more personalised way to stay informed, while the AI-powered photo retouching tools offer professional-grade editing capabilities within a user-friendly app. These enhancements not only improve the overall user experience but also demonstrate Apple's commitment to leveraging cutting-edge technology to make everyday tasks easier and more enjoyable. As users explore these new features, they will find that iOS 18 truly represents a significant leap forward in mobile technology.

Chapter 9: Safari and Web Browsing

Browsing Assistant: Summarizing Web Pages

Safari has always been at the forefront of web browsing innovation, and iOS 18 continues this tradition with the introduction of the Browsing Assistant. This feature is designed to make web browsing more efficient and user-friendly by summarizing web pages. Imagine having a personal assistant who can instantly condense long articles or complex information into digestible snippets – that's the power of Safari's Browsing Assistant.

The Power of Summarization

The Browsing Assistant uses advanced AI algorithms to analyze the content of a web page and extract its most important points.

This process involves parsing through text, identifying key sentences, and presenting a concise summary to the user. This is particularly useful for users who want to quickly grasp the essence of an article without wading through paragraphs of text.

For instance, if you're researching a topic and come across a lengthy academic paper, the Browsing Assistant can provide a brief overview of the paper's main arguments, findings, and conclusions. This allows you to determine whether the full text is worth a deeper dive, saving you valuable time and effort.

Practical Applications

The practical applications of the Browsing Assistant are vast. Students can use it to review academic articles and study materials more efficiently. Professionals can quickly scan through industry reports, news articles, and technical documents to stay informed about the latest trends and developments. Even casual readers can benefit from quick summaries of their favorite blogs or news sites, making it easier to keep up with a variety of content.

The Browsing Assistant isn't just limited to text-heavy pages. It can also summarize multimedia content, such as video transcripts and podcast summaries, providing a brief description of the main topics covered. This ensures that users get a comprehensive understanding of the content without necessarily engaging with it in full.

Enhancing User Experience

Safari's Browsing Assistant significantly enhances the user experience by reducing information overload. In today's fast-paced digital world, users are bombarded with vast amounts of information from various sources. The Browsing Assistant helps filter this information, allowing users to focus on what truly matters. By providing quick, accurate summaries, it empowers users to make informed decisions about which content to explore further.

The integration of the Browsing Assistant into Safari exemplifies Apple's commitment to leveraging AI for practical, user-centric applications. This feature not only streamlines web browsing but also aligns with broader trends in information consumption and digital literacy.

Page Eraser Tool: Removing Unwanted Web Page Portions

The Page Eraser Tool in Safari is another groundbreaking feature introduced in iOS 18, aimed at giving users more control over their web browsing experience. This tool allows users to remove unwanted portions of a web page, enhancing readability and customization.

Simplifying Web Content

The internet is a treasure trove of information, but it often comes with distractions such as ads, pop-ups, and irrelevant sections. The Page Eraser Tool enables users to declutter web pages by removing these distractions. With a simple click, users can erase advertisements, sidebars, or any other elements that detract from the main content.

For example, if you're reading an article but find the sidebars filled with ads and unrelated links, you can use the Page Eraser Tool to eliminate these elements, leaving you with a clean, focused reading experience. This not only improves readability but also reduces eye strain and enhances concentration.

Customizing Web Pages

Beyond simplifying content, the Page Eraser Tool offers customization options. Users can tailor web pages to suit their preferences, making them more aesthetically pleasing or easier to navigate. Whether it's removing excessive images, videos, or formatting elements, this tool puts the power of customization in the hands of the user.

This feature is particularly beneficial for individuals with specific accessibility needs. By removing or rearranging certain elements, users can create a more accessible web experience that aligns with their unique requirements. For instance, those with visual impairments can eliminate clutter that hinders screen reader functionality, making web content more navigable and understandable.

Streamlining Workflows

For professionals, the Page Eraser Tool can streamline workflows by allowing them to focus on the most relevant information. Researchers, writers, and analysts can use this tool to curate content that directly pertains to their work, removing extraneous material that may distract or confuse. This enhances productivity and ensures that users can access and utilize information more effectively.

In educational settings, teachers and students can use the Page Eraser Tool to create custom learning materials. Educators can strip down web pages to the essential information needed for lessons, while students can use the tool to focus on key points during their studies.

Enhancing Privacy

Another significant advantage of the Page Eraser Tool is its potential to enhance privacy. By removing tracking ads and scripts, users can reduce the amount of data collected about their browsing habits. This aligns with growing concerns about digital privacy and data security, offering users more control over their online presence.

The introduction of the Page Eraser Tool in Safari highlights Apple's dedication to improving user experience through innovative solutions. This feature empowers users to take control of their web browsing environment, making it more personalized, focused, and secure.

Intelligent Search: Identifying Key Topics and Phrases

Intelligent Search is a powerful feature in Safari that enhances the traditional search function by leveraging AI to identify key topics and phrases on web pages. This feature transforms how users interact with web content, making searches more precise and informative.

Advanced Search Capabilities

Intelligent Search goes beyond simple keyword matching. It uses natural language processing (NLP) to understand the context and relevance of words within a document. This allows Safari to provide more accurate and meaningful search results, helping users find the information they need more efficiently.

For example, if you're searching for information on climate change, Intelligent Search can highlight the most relevant sections of a web page, such as discussions on global warming, greenhouse gases, and policy impacts. This saves users the time and effort of sifting through entire articles to locate specific information.

Contextual Understanding

One of the standout features of Intelligent Search is its ability to understand the context in which keywords are used. This means that Safari can distinguish between different meanings of the same word based on the surrounding text. For instance, the word "apple" could refer to the fruit or the tech company. Intelligent Search can identify the appropriate context, ensuring that users receive the most relevant results.

This contextual understanding extends to complex queries as well. Users can input natural language questions, and Safari will interpret the query to deliver precise answers. This mimics the functionality of advanced search engines and virtual assistants, providing a seamless and intuitive search experience.

Enhancing Research and Learning

For students, researchers, and professionals, Intelligent Search is a game-changer. It facilitates deeper engagement with content by quickly pinpointing relevant information. This is particularly useful for academic research, where identifying key arguments and supporting evidence is crucial.

In educational settings, students can use Intelligent Search to extract important information from textbooks, articles, and research papers. This feature helps them study more effectively by focusing on the most pertinent content. Educators can also benefit by preparing lesson materials that highlight essential concepts and topics.

Boosting Productivity

Intelligent Search boosts productivity by minimizing the time spent on finding information. Whether you're conducting market research, writing a report, or simply browsing for personal interest, this feature streamlines the search process. By delivering precise and relevant results, it allows users to focus on analyzing and utilizing the information rather than searching for it.

Practical Applications

In the workplace, professionals can use Intelligent Search to navigate large volumes of documents and emails. This enhances efficiency and ensures that critical information is readily accessible. For instance, legal professionals can quickly locate key clauses in contracts, while marketers can identify trends and insights from industry reports.

Intelligent Search also integrates seamlessly with other iOS 18 features, such as the Browsing Assistant and Page Eraser Tool. This creates a cohesive and powerful web browsing experience that caters to the diverse needs of users.

Safari's enhancements in iOS 18, including the Browsing Assistant, Page Eraser Tool, and Intelligent Search, represent significant advancements in web browsing technology.

These features collectively enhance the user experience by making web content more accessible, customizable, and efficient.

The Browsing Assistant helps users quickly grasp the essence of web pages, while the Page Eraser Tool allows for a clutter-free and personalized browsing environment. Intelligent Search revolutionizes how users find and interact with information, making searches more accurate and contextually relevant.

Together, these features underscore Apple's commitment to leveraging AI for practical and user-centric applications. They not only improve the functionality of Safari but also align with broader trends in digital literacy, productivity, and privacy. As iOS 18 continues to evolve, users can look forward to an increasingly sophisticated and intuitive web browsing experience.

Chapter 10: System Settings and Accessibility

Settings App Redesign: Cleaner Interface and Improved Search

iOS 18 marks a pivotal point in the evolution of Apple's mobile operating system, particularly through the meticulous redesign of the Settings app. This revamp is not just a cosmetic upgrade; it's a reimagining of how users interact with their devices, offering a more intuitive, streamlined experience that significantly enhances usability.

Cleaner Interface

One of the most notable aspects of the Settings app redesign is its cleaner interface. Apple has adopted a minimalist approach, reducing visual clutter and making navigation more straightforward. This is immediately apparent upon opening the app, where users are greeted with a fresh, simplified layout.

The new design prioritizes essential functions and settings, presenting them in a way that is easy to understand and access. For example, instead of scrolling through endless menus, users now find key settings grouped logically into categories. This categorization is both intuitive and practical, allowing users to locate the settings they need with minimal effort.

The typography and iconography have also been updated, with a focus on clarity and readability. The use of larger, bold fonts and simple, clean icons helps users quickly identify different settings and options. Additionally, the color palette has been refined to offer better contrast and visual hierarchy, ensuring that important information stands out.

Improved Search Functionality

Another significant improvement in the Settings app is the enhanced search functionality. In previous versions, finding specific settings could sometimes be a frustrating experience, with users often struggling to remember the exact path to a particular option. iOS 18 addresses this issue head-on with a powerful new search feature.

The search bar, now prominently placed at the top of the Settings app, uses advanced AI algorithms to deliver more accurate and relevant results. This means that users can find what they are looking for with just a few keystrokes, rather than navigating through multiple layers of menus. For instance, typing in "Wi-Fi" instantly brings up all related settings, including network options, security preferences, and more.

The improved search also includes predictive text and suggestions. As users type, the search bar offers potential matches and shortcuts to frequently accessed settings. This not only speeds up the process of finding specific options but also helps users discover related settings they might not have been aware of.

Additionally, the search functionality is integrated with Siri, allowing users to perform searches using voice commands. By simply saying, "Hey Siri, open Wi-Fi settings," users can bypass manual searching altogether, making the process even more seamless and efficient.

User-Centric Design

At the core of these changes is a user-centric design philosophy. Apple has invested considerable effort into understanding how users interact with their devices and has tailored the Settings app to meet their needs. This approach is reflected in every aspect of the redesign, from the logical grouping of settings to the enhanced search capabilities.

Moreover, the Settings app now includes personalized suggestions based on individual usage patterns. For example, users who frequently adjust display settings might see quick access links to brightness and Night Shift controls on the main screen. This level of personalization ensures that the most relevant settings are always within easy reach, reducing the time and effort required to manage device preferences.

In conclusion, the redesign of the Settings app in iOS 18 is a masterclass in user-centric design. By focusing on a cleaner interface and improved search functionality, Apple has created a more intuitive and efficient experience for users. These changes not only make it easier to navigate and manage device settings but also highlight Apple's commitment to continuous improvement and innovation.

New Accessibility Features

iOS 18 takes accessibility to new heights, introducing a range of features designed to make Apple's devices more inclusive and user-friendly. These enhancements reflect Apple's ongoing commitment to providing a seamless and empowering experience for all users, regardless of their abilities.

Enhanced Voice Control

One of the standout accessibility features in iOS 18 is the enhanced Voice Control. This feature allows users to navigate their devices and perform various tasks using only their voice. Building on the success of previous versions, the new Voice Control is more accurate and responsive, thanks to advanced speech recognition algorithms.

Users can now dictate text, control apps, and navigate through the operating system with greater ease. For instance, commands like "Open Mail," "Scroll down," or "Tap Send" can be executed seamlessly, providing a hands-free experience that is both efficient and empowering. This is particularly beneficial for users with mobility impairments, who may find traditional touch-based interactions challenging.

Real-Time Text (RTT)

Another significant addition is the Real-Time Text (RTT) feature, which allows users to send text messages during phone calls. This is particularly useful for individuals who are deaf or hard of hearing, as it provides a real-time communication method that complements voice and video calls.

RTT is seamlessly integrated into the Phone app, enabling users to switch between text and voice communication without interrupting the call. This ensures that conversations are fluid and inclusive, accommodating a wider range of communication preferences and needs.

Magnifier App Enhancements

The Magnifier app, which turns the iPhone into a powerful digital magnifying glass, has also received notable upgrades. In iOS 18, the app includes a new Reader mode, which makes it easier to read text on the screen. This mode enhances contrast, adjusts text size, and simplifies the layout, making it more accessible for users with visual impairments.

Additionally, the Magnifier app now supports multiple filters and color adjustments, allowing users to customize the viewing experience to suit their specific needs. These enhancements ensure that users can comfortably read and interact with digital content, regardless of their visual capabilities.

AssistiveTouch and Custom Gestures

AssistiveTouch, a feature designed to help users with motor skill impairments, has been further refined in iOS 18. Users can now create custom gestures and shortcuts, making it easier to perform complex tasks with a single tap. This includes multi-step actions, such as opening an app and performing a specific task within it.

The ability to customize gestures and actions means that users can tailor their device interactions to match their unique needs and preferences. This level of personalization is a testament to Apple's commitment to providing an inclusive and flexible user experience.

Improved Hearing Aid Support

iOS 18 also brings improvements to hearing aid support, ensuring that users with hearing impairments have a seamless and high-quality audio experience. The operating system now includes enhanced compatibility with a wider range of hearing aids and cochlear implants, providing better sound quality and more reliable connectivity.

Additionally, the Hearing section in the Settings app offers new customization options, allowing users to adjust audio settings to match their hearing profiles. This includes features like Live Listen, which uses the iPhone's microphone to amplify sound, making it easier to hear conversations and ambient sounds in noisy environments.

Expanded Accessibility Shortcuts

Accessibility shortcuts have been expanded in iOS 18, providing quicker and easier access to essential features. Users can now customize the shortcuts menu, adding frequently used accessibility options for instant access. This includes features like VoiceOver, Magnifier, AssistiveTouch, and more.

By making these shortcuts easily accessible, Apple ensures that users can quickly enable and adjust accessibility features as needed, without navigating through multiple menus. This enhances the overall user experience, making it more convenient and efficient.

The new accessibility features in iOS 18 underscore Apple's dedication to inclusivity and innovation. By enhancing Voice Control, introducing Real-Time Text, upgrading the Magnifier app, refining AssistiveTouch, improving hearing aid support, and expanding accessibility shortcuts, Apple has created a more accessible and user-friendly operating system.

These features not only make it easier for users with disabilities to interact with their devices but also highlight Apple's commitment to creating technology that empowers and enriches the lives of all users. iOS 18 sets a new standard for accessibility, demonstrating that thoughtful design and advanced technology can create a more inclusive digital world.

Chapter 11: Automation and Shortcuts

Shortcuts App: Easier Automation of Complex Tasks

In an age where efficiency is paramount, Apple's Shortcuts app emerges as a game-changer, revolutionizing how users interact with their devices. This chapter delves into the transformative power of the Shortcuts app, exploring its capabilities, ease of use, and the immense potential it holds for automating complex tasks. From simplifying daily routines to executing multi-step processes seamlessly, the Shortcuts app is designed to enhance productivity and make your iOS experience more intuitive and enjoyable.

The Power of Automation

Automation has long been the cornerstone of technological advancement. By delegating repetitive or intricate tasks to automated processes, users can focus on more meaningful activities. The Shortcuts app exemplifies this principle, offering a robust platform for creating custom workflows that integrate seamlessly with the iOS ecosystem. Whether you're an average user looking to save time or a tech-savvy individual aiming to push the boundaries of what your device can do, the Shortcuts app caters to a wide spectrum of needs.

Getting Started with Shortcuts

The Shortcuts app, available on iOS devices, provides an intuitive interface for creating and managing automation workflows. Upon launching the app, users are greeted with a library of pre-built shortcuts, showcasing the app's versatility. These pre-built shortcuts serve as excellent starting points, illustrating the various ways automation can enhance daily tasks. Users can also create their own shortcuts from scratch, tailoring them to specific needs and preferences.

To begin, simply tap the "Create Shortcut" button. This opens a blank canvas where you can start building your workflow by adding actions. Actions are the building blocks of shortcuts, each representing a single step in the process. The app supports a wide range of actions, from sending messages and emails to controlling smart home devices and retrieving data from the web. By stringing together multiple actions, users can create powerful automation sequences that perform complex tasks with a single tap or voice command.

Real-World Applications: Streamlining Daily Routines

One of the most compelling uses of the Shortcuts app is streamlining daily routines. Consider a morning routine that involves checking the weather, setting reminders for the day, and playing your favorite playlist. With Shortcuts, you can automate all these actions into a single workflow. A simple voice command like "Good morning" can trigger the shortcut, which fetches the latest weather report, lists your reminders, and starts playing your music—all without requiring manual input for each task.

Enhancing Productivity

For professionals, the Shortcuts app can significantly enhance productivity. Imagine a scenario where you need to send a daily status report to your team. Instead of manually composing the email each day, you can create a shortcut that gathers data from various sources, formats it into a structured email, and sends it to the designated recipients. This not only saves time but also ensures consistency and accuracy in your communications.

Smart Home Integration

The integration of smart home devices with the Shortcuts app opens up a realm of possibilities for home automation. You can create shortcuts that adjust the thermostat, turn off the lights, and lock the doors when you say, "Goodnight." Similarly, arriving home can trigger a shortcut that turns on the lights, adjusts the thermostat, and plays relaxing music. The ability to control multiple devices with a single command enhances convenience and provides a seamless smart home experience.

Customizing Shortcuts

Customization is at the heart of the Shortcuts app. Users can personalize shortcuts to fit their unique workflows and preferences. This includes setting parameters for actions, adding conditional logic, and incorporating variables. For instance, a shortcut for sending a message can include a prompt for the user to enter a custom message each time it runs. Conditional logic allows shortcuts to make decisions based on certain criteria, such as the time of day or the user's location, further enhancing their flexibility and utility.

Advanced Features: Scripting and Variables

For users who want to delve deeper into automation, the Shortcuts app offers advanced features like scripting and variables. Scripting actions enable shortcuts to perform more complex operations, such as running loops, making calculations, and interacting with web APIs. Variables allow shortcuts to store and manipulate data, making them more dynamic and capable of handling a broader range of tasks. For example, a shortcut can retrieve the user's current location, perform a web search for nearby restaurants, and display the results in a formatted list.

Integration with Third-Party Apps

The Shortcuts app's integration with third-party apps extends its capabilities beyond the built-in iOS features. Many popular apps provide shortcut actions that can be incorporated into workflows. For instance, you can create a shortcut that logs your daily exercise data from a fitness app, sends a summary to your health coach, and updates your progress on a shared spreadsheet. This level of integration fosters a more interconnected and efficient digital ecosystem.

Sharing and Discovering Shortcuts

The Shortcuts app community plays a significant role in its success. Users can share their custom shortcuts with others, fostering a collaborative environment where ideas and workflows are exchanged. Apple's Shortcuts Gallery features a curated collection of shortcuts created by the community, providing inspiration and practical solutions for common tasks. By exploring and customizing these shared shortcuts, users can continually expand their automation repertoire.

Security and Privacy

As with all Apple products, security and privacy are paramount in the Shortcuts app. Shortcuts that access sensitive data or perform critical actions require explicit user permission, ensuring that your information remains secure. Additionally, the app's on-device processing minimizes the risk of data breaches, as all operations are performed locally rather than in the cloud. This approach aligns with Apple's commitment to user privacy, providing peace of mind while using powerful automation features.

The Shortcuts app represents a significant leap forward in personal and professional productivity. By harnessing the power of automation, users can simplify their lives, streamline their workflows, and unlock new levels of efficiency. Whether you're automating mundane tasks or creating complex multi-step processes, the Shortcuts app empowers you to do more with your iOS device. As technology continues to evolve, the possibilities for automation are boundless, making the Shortcuts app an indispensable tool in the digital age.

Chapter 12: Siri's Advanced Capabilities

Generative AI and Natural Conversations

Text and Image Generation

Siri, Apple's virtual assistant, has come a long way since its inception, evolving from a simple voice command tool into a sophisticated AI companion. With iOS 18, Siri takes a significant leap forward, leveraging generative AI to enhance its conversational abilities. At the core of this transformation is Siri's newfound capability to generate text and images, a feature that brings a new dimension to user interactions.

Generative AI allows Siri to produce natural, contextually relevant text responses. For instance, when users ask Siri to draft a message or an email, it can now generate a coherent, professional-sounding text that aligns with the user's tone and intent. This advancement is powered by large language models that have been trained on vast datasets, enabling Siri to understand nuances and subtleties in language. Imagine dictating a business email while on the go; Siri can now craft a polished message that captures your thoughts accurately, saving you time and effort.

In addition to text generation, Siri's capabilities extend to image creation. Utilizing AI-driven algorithms, Siri can generate custom images based on user descriptions. For example, if a user needs a specific type of graphic for a presentation or a social media post, Siri can create an image that fits the criteria. This feature is particularly useful for content creators and professionals who need quick, high-quality visuals without the hassle of manual design work.

The integration of text and image generation into Siri's repertoire not only enhances productivity but also makes interactions more engaging and dynamic. Users can rely on Siri to handle complex tasks that require creativity and precision, transforming the way they approach everyday activities.

Personalized Responses

One of the standout features of Siri in iOS 18 is its ability to deliver personalized responses. This enhancement is rooted in advanced AI that learns from user interactions to provide tailored assistance. Siri now considers the context of previous conversations, user preferences, and even individual habits to offer more relevant and useful responses.

Personalization goes beyond simple command execution. For instance, when you ask Siri for restaurant recommendations, it takes into account your past dining preferences, favorite cuisines, and even your current location to suggest places you're likely to enjoy. This level of customization makes Siri feel more like a personal assistant who understands your unique tastes and needs.

The personalization extends to task management as well. When setting reminders or scheduling events, Siri can suggest optimal times based on your routine, ensuring that you stay organized without feeling overwhelmed. Additionally, Siri can now recognize the voices of different users on the same device, providing a customized experience for each family member. This multi-user support is particularly beneficial in households where several people share a single device, as it ensures that everyone receives personalized assistance tailored to their individual preferences.

By combining generative AI with personalized responses, Siri in iOS 18 sets a new standard for virtual assistants. It offers a seamless, intuitive user experience that adapts to individual needs, making daily tasks easier and more enjoyable.

Future Enhancements: Per-App Controls Planned for 2025

Looking ahead, Apple has ambitious plans for Siri, with per-app controls expected to roll out in 2025. This future enhancement will revolutionize how users interact with Siri, providing greater flexibility and control over app-specific functions.

Per-app controls will allow users to customize how Siri interacts with different applications. For example, you might configure Siri to provide detailed sports updates from your favorite sports app, while keeping notifications from other apps brief and to the point. This level of customization ensures that Siri's assistance is aligned with your specific needs and preferences for each app, enhancing the overall user experience.

Moreover, per-app controls will enable developers to integrate Siri more deeply into their applications. This means that third-party apps can offer unique voice-controlled features that leverage Siri's advanced capabilities. For instance, a fitness app might allow users to start specific workouts, track progress, and receive personalized coaching tips, all through voice commands. Similarly, a shopping app could enable users to browse products, place orders, and check delivery status, making the entire shopping experience more convenient and hands-free.

The introduction of per-app controls also promises to enhance accessibility. Users with disabilities will benefit from tailored voice interactions that simplify navigation and control within their favorite apps. By enabling more granular control over app functions, Siri can provide a more inclusive and empowering experience for all users.

In addition to these user-centric enhancements, per-app controls will bolster security and privacy. Users will have the ability to manage Siri's access to sensitive data within specific apps, ensuring that their information remains protected. Apple's commitment to on-device processing means that most interactions with Siri will continue to occur locally, safeguarding user data from potential breaches.

As we look to the future, the evolution of Siri with per-app controls is poised to redefine the role of virtual assistants. This development will make Siri an even more integral part of the iOS ecosystem, offering unprecedented levels of customization, convenience, and security. Whether you're managing your daily schedule, controlling smart home devices, or interacting with your favorite apps, Siri's advanced capabilities will ensure a seamless, personalized experience that enhances every aspect of your digital life.

The advancements in Siri with iOS 18 and beyond underscore Apple's commitment to innovation and user-centric design. By harnessing the power of generative AI and introducing personalized responses, Siri has become a more intuitive and capable assistant. The future enhancements, including per-app controls, promise to further elevate the user experience, making Siri an indispensable tool in navigating the complexities of modern life. As we embrace these technological advancements, one thing is clear: Siri is not just keeping pace with the future; it's shaping it.

Chapter 13: Improved Search and Voice Features

Spotlight Search: Smarter Results and Sorting

Spotlight Search in iOS 18 represents a significant leap forward in how users interact with their devices. Traditionally, Spotlight has served as a useful tool for quickly finding apps, contacts, emails, and other data on your iPhone or iPad. However, with the integration of advanced AI and machine learning technologies, Spotlight in iOS 18 is set to become an indispensable feature that revolutionizes the way we search for information.

One of the most exciting enhancements in Spotlight Search is the introduction of smarter results and sorting. This upgrade ensures that the search results are not only more relevant but also intelligently sorted based on context and user behavior. When you perform a search in iOS 18, Spotlight will analyze various factors such as your recent activities, app usage patterns, and even the time of day to deliver the most pertinent results.

For instance, if you frequently search for your calendar events in the morning, Spotlight will prioritize displaying your daily schedule when you initiate a search during that time. Similarly, if you often look up a particular contact in the evening, Spotlight will recognize this pattern and bring that contact to the top of your search results. This context-aware sorting mechanism saves time and enhances productivity by ensuring that you get what you need without sifting through irrelevant results.

The improved sorting capabilities extend beyond simple contextual awareness. Spotlight in iOS 18 also employs advanced natural language processing (NLP) to understand the nuances of your queries better. This means that even if you type in a search phrase in a slightly different manner each time, Spotlight can still interpret your intent and provide accurate results. For example, whether you search for "photos from last summer" or "summer 2023 pictures," Spotlight will understand that you are looking for images from the same period and display them accordingly.

Additionally, the integration of AI allows Spotlight to surface related content that you might not have explicitly searched for but could find useful. For example, if you search for a specific project file, Spotlight might also show recent emails, notes, or calendar events related to that project. This holistic approach to search results ensures that you have access to a comprehensive set of information, enhancing your ability to make informed decisions quickly.

Another notable feature is the predictive search suggestions. As you start typing in the search bar, Spotlight will proactively suggest potential queries based on your past searches and current context. This feature not only speeds up the search process but also introduces a level of convenience that makes the user experience more fluid and intuitive.

The visual presentation of search results has also been revamped. Spotlight now categorizes results into distinct sections, such as apps, contacts, emails, documents, and web results, making it easier to navigate through the information. This organized layout ensures that you can quickly locate the desired result without feeling overwhelmed by a long list of ungrouped items.

Moreover, the integration of on-device processing ensures that your search data remains private and secure. Unlike cloud-based search engines that might transmit your queries to external servers, Spotlight in iOS 18 performs most of its operations locally on your device. This approach not only enhances privacy but also speeds up the search process by reducing reliance on external networks.

In summary, the smarter results and sorting capabilities of Spotlight Search in iOS 18 mark a significant advancement in how users interact with their devices. By leveraging AI and machine learning, Spotlight delivers highly relevant, context-aware search results that are intelligently sorted and presented in an organized manner. This enhanced functionality transforms Spotlight from a simple search tool into a powerful assistant that anticipates your needs and streamlines your workflow.

Real-Time Audio Transcription

Voice Memos has long been a go-to app for quickly recording thoughts, lectures, interviews, and other audio snippets. With iOS 18, Voice Memos undergoes a transformative upgrade, introducing real-time audio transcription capabilities that bring a new level of utility and professionalism to the app.

Real-time audio transcription in Voice Memos means that as you record, the app simultaneously converts spoken words into text. This feature is particularly beneficial for users who need to capture and review spoken content quickly and accurately. Whether you're a journalist conducting an interview, a student recording a lecture, or a professional documenting meeting notes, real-time transcription makes it easier to organize and reference your recordings.

One of the standout aspects of this feature is its accuracy. Leveraging advanced speech recognition algorithms and AI, Voice

Memos can accurately transcribe spoken words, even in environments with background noise. The transcription process is not only fast but also highly reliable, ensuring that the text output closely matches the spoken input. This high level of accuracy is crucial for maintaining the integrity of the recorded information and reducing the need for manual corrections.

The real-time transcription feature also includes speaker identification, which is especially useful in scenarios involving multiple speakers. During an interview or meeting, for instance, the app can distinguish between different voices and label them accordingly in the transcription. This differentiation helps in attributing statements to the correct individuals, making the transcription more organized and easier to follow.

Furthermore, the transcriptions are time-stamped, allowing users to easily navigate through the audio file. By clicking on a specific section of the text, you can jump directly to that point in the recording. This functionality is invaluable for reviewing key moments or quotes without having to listen to the entire audio file. It enhances efficiency and ensures that you can quickly locate and revisit important parts of the recording.

The integration of real-time transcription into Voice Memos also opens up new possibilities for accessibility. For users with hearing impairments, the ability to see a text representation of spoken content in real-time makes the app more inclusive. It also benefits individuals who prefer reading over listening, providing a versatile way to consume and interact with recorded information.

Voice Memos in iOS 18 also supports editing and annotating transcriptions. After a recording session, you can review the text, make necessary edits, and add notes or comments directly within the app. This feature is particularly useful for adding context, clarifying points, or summarizing key takeaways. The ability to annotate transcriptions enhances the overall utility of the app, turning it into a comprehensive tool for capturing, reviewing, and managing audio content.

The enhanced search functionality within Voice Memos further complements the transcription feature. Users can search for specific words or phrases within their transcriptions, making it easier to find relevant information across multiple recordings. This powerful search capability transforms Voice Memos into a searchable repository of audio content, significantly improving productivity and information retrieval.

In terms of privacy and security, Apple continues to prioritize user data protection.

The real-time transcription feature processes audio data on-device, ensuring that sensitive information remains private and secure. This local processing approach aligns with Apple's commitment to safeguarding user data and maintaining trust.

In conclusion, the introduction of real-time audio transcription in Voice Memos elevates the app to a new level of functionality and convenience. By providing accurate, speaker-identified, and time-stamped transcriptions, the app enhances the way users capture, review, and manage audio content. The ability to edit, annotate, and search transcriptions further solidifies Voice Memos as an essential tool for professionals, students, and anyone who relies on recorded information. With these enhancements, Voice Memos in iOS 18 stands out as a powerful and versatile app that caters to a wide range of needs while maintaining the highest standards of privacy and accuracy.

Chapter 14: Technological Advancements in iOS 18

Integration of Augmented Reality

The world of technology is ever-evolving, and with each new iteration of Apple's iOS, users are treated to a plethora of innovative features designed to enhance their digital experiences. iOS 18 is no exception, pushing the boundaries of what's possible with mobile technology. One of the most groundbreaking advancements in this release is the deep integration of Augmented Reality (AR), transforming the way users interact with their environment and digital content.

The Dawn of a New Reality

Augmented Reality has been a buzzword in the tech industry for several years, but with iOS 18, Apple is making AR more accessible and useful than ever before. By blending digital elements with the physical world, AR creates immersive experiences that were once the realm of science fiction. Whether it's gaming, education, shopping, or navigation, AR's potential is being realized in myriad ways.

ARKit 5: The Backbone of Augmented Reality

At the heart of iOS 18's AR capabilities is ARKit 5, Apple's latest iteration of its powerful AR development framework. ARKit 5 introduces a host of new features that make it easier for developers to create sophisticated AR experiences. One of the standout features is improved motion tracking, which allows for more precise and realistic interactions between digital objects and the real world. This means smoother animations, more accurate placement of virtual objects, and a more engaging user experience.

Real-World Applications

The applications of AR in iOS 18 are vast and varied. In retail, for instance, AR allows users to visualize products in their own space before making a purchase. Imagine being able to see how a new piece of furniture would look in your living room, or how a pair of shoes would match your outfit, all from the comfort of your home. This not only enhances the shopping experience but also reduces the likelihood of returns, benefiting both consumers and retailers.

In education, AR is revolutionizing the way students learn. Interactive textbooks come to life with 3D models that can be manipulated and explored, making complex subjects like biology or astronomy more tangible and understandable. Teachers can create dynamic lessons that engage students in ways traditional methods cannot match.

Enhancing Navigation and Exploration

Navigation is another area where AR is making significant strides. With iOS 18, Apple Maps integrates AR to provide more intuitive and accurate directions. Instead of looking at a flat map, users can see arrows and instructions overlaid on the real world through their device's camera, making it easier to navigate unfamiliar places. This feature is particularly useful in large, complex environments like airports, malls, and universities.

Gaming and Entertainment

Of course, AR's impact on gaming and entertainment cannot be overstated. iOS 18 takes mobile gaming to new heights, offering immersive experiences that blur the line between the digital and physical worlds. Games can now utilize the user's surroundings, turning everyday environments into fantastical landscapes. This level of immersion enhances gameplay and offers new ways for players to interact with the game world.

The Future of AR

As developers continue to explore the possibilities of ARKit 5, the potential for innovative applications will only grow. From virtual try-ons and interactive learning to enhanced navigation and immersive gaming, AR is poised to become an integral part of our daily lives. With iOS 18, Apple is leading the charge, ensuring that users have access to the most advanced and engaging AR experiences available.

Introduction to Swift Programming Language

As Apple continues to push the boundaries of technology with each new iteration of iOS, it also provides developers with the tools they need to create groundbreaking applications. One of the most powerful tools in a developer's arsenal is Swift, Apple's modern programming language designed specifically for building iOS, macOS, watchOS, and tvOS applications. With iOS 18, Swift remains at the forefront, empowering developers to bring their ideas to life with greater ease and efficiency.

The Genesis of Swift

Introduced by Apple in 2014, Swift was designed to be a powerful and intuitive programming language that offers the best of both worlds: the performance of compiled languages and the simplicity of scripting languages. Swift is fast, secure, and expressive, making it the preferred choice for many developers working within the Apple ecosystem.

Swift's Core Principles

Swift was built with several core principles in mind, all aimed at improving the developer experience:

- *Safety*: Swift eliminates entire classes of unsafe code. For example, it manages memory automatically, preventing many common programming errors.

- *Performance*: Swift is designed to be fast, with performance comparable to C-based languages. This means apps built with Swift can run efficiently on all Apple devices.

- *Expressiveness*: Swift's syntax is concise yet expressive, allowing developers to write clean, readable code. Features like type inference and modern control flow make coding more intuitive and less error-prone.

- *Interoperability*: Swift is fully interoperable with Objective-C, allowing developers to integrate Swift code into existing projects seamlessly.

Learning Swift

For new developers, learning Swift is an exciting journey. Apple provides extensive resources to help beginners get started, including interactive tutorials, comprehensive documentation, and a vibrant developer community. The Swift Playgrounds app, available on iPad and Mac, offers a fun and interactive way to learn the basics of Swift through guided exercises and challenges.

Advanced Features

For experienced developers, Swift offers advanced features that enable the creation of complex and high-performance applications:

- *Optionals*: Swift's type system includes optionals, which make it clear when a value can be absent. This helps prevent runtime errors and makes the code more predictable.

- *Closures*: Swift's closures (similar to lambdas or anonymous functions in other languages) provide a way to encapsulate functionality and pass it around in your code.

- *Generics*: Generics allow developers to write flexible and reusable functions and types that can work with any data type.

- *Protocol-Oriented Programming*: Swift embraces protocol-oriented programming, which encourages the use of protocols to define interfaces and behavior, promoting code reuse and flexibility.

Swift and iOS 18

With iOS 18, Swift continues to evolve, introducing new features and improvements that enhance developer productivity and app performance. One notable addition is the enhanced concurrency model, which simplifies the development of asynchronous code. This is crucial for creating responsive apps that can handle multiple tasks simultaneously without compromising performance.

Opportunities for Developers

iOS 18 opens up a world of opportunities for developers. The integration of advanced technologies like augmented reality, machine learning, and artificial intelligence allows developers to create innovative applications that were previously unimaginable. With Swift and the powerful tools provided by Apple, developers can harness these technologies to deliver unique and engaging experiences to users.

Community and Support

The Swift community is one of the most vibrant and supportive in the tech industry. Developers can connect with peers, share knowledge, and collaborate on projects through forums, meetups, and online platforms like GitHub. Apple also hosts the annual Worldwide Developers Conference (WWDC), where developers can learn about the latest advancements in Swift and iOS, attend workshops, and network with other professionals.

The Future of Swift

As technology continues to advance, Swift will remain a crucial tool for developers working within the Apple ecosystem. Its combination of performance, safety, and expressiveness makes it ideal for building the next generation of applications. With ongoing updates and a strong community, Swift is well-positioned to support developers in creating innovative and impactful apps for years to come.

We have explored the technological advancements in iOS 18, focusing on the integration of augmented reality and the opportunities presented by Swift, Apple's powerful programming language. As AR transforms the way we interact with the world and Swift empowers developers to create exceptional applications, iOS 18 stands as a testament to Apple's commitment to innovation and excellence. Whether you're a user enjoying the new features or a developer bringing your vision to life, iOS 18 offers an exciting glimpse into the future of mobile technology.

Chapter 15: iOS 18 in Education and Business

Impact on Classroom Learning

In recent years, technology has increasingly become an integral part of education. With the introduction of iOS 18, Apple is taking a giant leap forward in enhancing classroom learning experiences. The operating system's new features and improvements are designed to provide a more interactive, engaging, and efficient learning environment for both students and educators.

One of the standout features of iOS 18 is its enhanced augmented reality (AR) capabilities. AR has the potential to transform the way students learn by bringing subjects to life in ways that traditional methods cannot. For instance, a biology class can use AR to explore the human body in 3D, allowing students to see and interact with organs and systems in a virtual environment. This hands-on approach can help to deepen understanding and retention of complex concepts.

The integration of AI and machine learning in iOS 18 also plays a crucial role in personalizing education. Siri, Apple's virtual assistant, has become smarter and more intuitive, capable of assisting students with their studies in a more meaningful way. For example, Siri can now help students with their homework by providing step-by-step explanations of math problems or summarizing historical events. This kind of personalized assistance can cater to the unique learning pace and style of each student, making education more inclusive and effective.

Additionally, the new Freeform app in iOS 18 introduces a feature called "Scenes," which simplifies navigation within large boards. This is particularly useful for collaborative projects and brainstorming sessions. Teachers can create interactive lesson plans and digital boards where students can contribute ideas, share resources, and work together in real-time, regardless of their physical location. This fosters a collaborative learning environment that encourages creativity and critical thinking.

iOS 18 also enhances the Classroom app, which is a powerful tool for teachers to manage their classes. The updated app includes features that allow teachers to monitor student progress, distribute assignments, and provide instant feedback more efficiently. For example, teachers can see what each student is working on, guide them through tasks, and even lock apps or devices to keep students focused. This level of control and oversight helps to maintain a structured and productive classroom environment.

Furthermore, the improved integration between the Calendar and Reminders apps makes it easier for students and teachers to manage their schedules and assignments. Students can set reminders for homework deadlines, test dates, and project submissions, while teachers can schedule classes, meetings, and school events. This seamless organization helps to reduce the stress associated with academic responsibilities and ensures that important tasks are not overlooked.

Another significant improvement in iOS 18 is the increased accessibility features, which are particularly beneficial in an educational setting. Features such as VoiceOver, Magnifier, and new text-to-speech options make learning more accessible for students with disabilities. These tools ensure that all students, regardless of their physical or cognitive abilities, have equal opportunities to succeed in their studies.

Overall, iOS 18's advancements in AR, AI, collaboration tools, and accessibility are set to revolutionize classroom learning. By creating a more interactive, personalized, and inclusive educational environment, Apple is empowering students and teachers to achieve their full potential.

Sustainability Initiatives: Reduced Carbon Footprint

Apple has long been committed to environmental sustainability, and with iOS 18, the company is furthering its efforts to reduce the carbon footprint of its devices and operations. This latest operating system is designed with energy efficiency and environmental consciousness in mind, reflecting Apple's dedication to making technology that is not only innovative but also sustainable.

One of the key sustainability initiatives in iOS 18 is the optimization of battery usage. The new operating system includes advanced power management features that help to extend battery life and reduce energy consumption. For example, iOS 18 intelligently adjusts background activities and resource allocation based on usage patterns, ensuring that power is used efficiently without compromising performance. This not only benefits users by providing longer battery life but also contributes to reducing the overall energy consumption of millions of devices worldwide.

In addition to power management, iOS 18 introduces new features that promote environmentally friendly practices. The operating system includes enhanced support for low-power modes and energy-saving settings, allowing users to minimize their devices' environmental impact. For instance, the new Low Power Mode in iOS

18 reduces the energy consumption of apps and services when the battery level is low, helping to conserve power and reduce the frequency of charging.

Apple's commitment to sustainability extends beyond software to the hardware and manufacturing processes as well. The company has made significant strides in using recycled materials in its products, and iOS 18 is designed to support these eco-friendly devices. For example, the operating system includes features that optimize the performance of devices made with recycled materials, ensuring that they deliver the same high-quality user experience as new products. This helps to reduce the demand for raw materials and decrease the environmental impact of manufacturing.

Furthermore, iOS 18 supports Apple's broader initiatives to reduce its carbon footprint across its supply chain and operations. The company has set ambitious goals to achieve carbon neutrality for its entire business, including its products and supply chain, by 2030. This involves using 100% recycled and renewable materials in its products, investing in renewable energy projects, and improving energy efficiency in its operations. iOS 18 plays a crucial role in these efforts by enabling devices to operate more efficiently and sustainably.

Apple also encourages developers to adopt sustainable practices through the App Store and its development tools. With iOS 18, the company provides developers with resources and guidelines for creating energy-efficient apps that minimize their environmental impact. This includes optimizing app performance, reducing energy consumption, and utilizing iOS 18's power management features. By promoting sustainable app development, Apple is fostering a culture of environmental responsibility within the tech industry.

Moreover, iOS 18 includes new features that help users make more environmentally conscious decisions. For example, the operating system provides detailed information about the environmental impact of apps and services, allowing users to choose options that align with their sustainability goals. This transparency empowers users to take an active role in reducing their carbon footprint and supports Apple's mission to create a more sustainable future.

In conclusion, iOS 18's sustainability initiatives and reduced carbon footprint reflect Apple's ongoing commitment to environmental responsibility. By optimizing energy efficiency, promoting the use of recycled materials, and encouraging sustainable practices among developers and users, Apple is paving the way for a greener and more sustainable tech industry. Through these efforts, iOS 18 not only delivers innovative and powerful features but also contributes to a healthier planet for future generations.

Chapter 16: Future Trends and Speculations

Predictions for iOS 19

As technology continues to evolve at a breakneck pace, so too does Apple's iOS. Each iteration brings with it a suite of innovative features, enhancements, and improvements that push the boundaries of what our devices can do. With the groundbreaking updates in iOS 18 setting a high bar, tech enthusiasts and industry insiders are eagerly speculating about what iOS 19 might bring to the table. In this chapter, we delve into some of the most exciting predictions for iOS 19, exploring potential advancements in AI, augmented reality, user interface, and more.

1. Advanced Artificial Intelligence Integration

One of the most anticipated advancements in iOS 19 is the further integration of artificial intelligence (AI) across the system. Building on the foundations laid by iOS 18, which introduced significant AI-powered features, iOS 19 is expected to take this to the next level.

Enhanced Siri Capabilities

Siri, Apple's virtual assistant, has seen substantial improvements over the years, but there is always room for growth. iOS 19 could see Siri becoming even more intuitive and capable, leveraging advancements in machine learning and natural language processing. This might include:

- *Contextual Understanding*: Siri could become better at understanding context, allowing for more fluid and natural conversations. For example, if you ask Siri about your plans for the weekend, it could automatically refer to your calendar and suggest relevant activities or reminders.

- *Proactive Assistance*: Siri might become more proactive, offering suggestions and performing tasks without being explicitly asked. Imagine Siri reminding you to leave for a meeting based on current traffic conditions or suggesting workout routines based on your activity levels.

Intelligent Personalization

iOS 19 could further enhance personalization, making your device even more tailored to your needs and preferences. AI could analyze your habits, preferences, and usage patterns to provide a more customized experience. This might manifest in:

- *Smart Notifications*: Notifications could be prioritized based on their importance and your past interactions. For instance, messages from close contacts or critical app alerts could be highlighted, while less important notifications are minimized.

- *Dynamic Home Screen*: Your home screen layout could dynamically adjust based on your usage patterns, surfacing frequently used apps and widgets when you need them most.

2. *Augmented Reality and Mixed Reality Enhancements*

Apple has been steadily investing in augmented reality (AR) technologies, and iOS 19 is expected to bring even more robust AR capabilities to the platform.

ARKit Improvements

ARKit, Apple's augmented reality development framework, is likely to see significant upgrades. These could include:

- *More Realistic AR Experiences:* Enhanced rendering techniques and improved object tracking could make AR experiences more immersive and realistic. This might involve better integration of virtual objects into real-world environments, with more accurate lighting, shadows, and occlusion.

- *Expanded Developer Tools*: New tools and APIs could empower developers to create even more sophisticated AR applications, ranging from gaming and entertainment to education and productivity.

Mixed Reality Features

Beyond augmented reality, iOS 19 might introduce mixed reality (MR) features that blend the physical and digital worlds more seamlessly. This could include:

- *Interactive Environments*: Users could interact with virtual elements in their physical space in more meaningful ways.

For example, virtual furniture could be placed in your living room and interact with real-world objects, providing a more accurate preview of how it would look and fit.

- *Enhanced Wearables Integration:* With rumors of Apple developing AR glasses, iOS 19 could include features specifically designed to enhance the experience of using wearables. This might involve displaying contextual information and notifications directly in your field of view, creating a more immersive and hands-free experience.

3. User Interface and Experience Overhaul

Apple has always been known for its attention to design and user experience, and iOS 19 is expected to continue this tradition with several user interface (UI) and experience (UX) enhancements.

Dynamic and Adaptive UI

The UI of iOS 19 might become more dynamic and adaptive, adjusting to different contexts and usage scenarios. This could include:

- *Contextual Menus:* Menus and options that dynamically adjust based on the current context, providing relevant options without cluttering the interface. For example, long-pressing on an app icon might present different options based on the app's current state or your recent activity.

- *Enhanced Customization*: More options for customizing the look and feel of the OS, including themes, icon packs, and layout adjustments. Users might be able to create their own custom themes or download them from a marketplace.

Improved Accessibility Features

Apple has always prioritized accessibility, and iOS 19 is expected to introduce new features to make the OS even more inclusive:

- *Voice Control Enhancements:* Improved voice control options that allow users to navigate and control their device entirely through voice commands. This might include more natural language processing capabilities and better integration with third-party apps.

- *Advanced Assistive Technologies*: New assistive technologies that provide better support for users with disabilities. For example, enhanced screen readers, haptic feedback options, and more customizable accessibility settings.

4. *Privacy and Security Enhancements*

Privacy and security have always been cornerstones of iOS, and iOS 19 is expected to introduce new features to keep user data safe and secure.

Enhanced Data Privacy

iOS 19 could include more robust privacy features to give users greater control over their data:

- *Granular Permissions*: More granular control over app permissions, allowing users to specify exactly what data each app can access. For example, you might be able to allow an app to access your location only when it's actively being used, or to access certain data types but not others.

- *Privacy Reports*: Detailed privacy reports that provide insights into how apps are using your data. These reports could highlight potential privacy risks and offer suggestions for improving your data security.

Advanced Security Features

Security enhancements in iOS 19 might include:

- *Biometric Security Improvements*: Enhanced facial recognition and fingerprint scanning technologies for faster and more secure authentication. This could involve more accurate detection of spoofing attempts and better support for wearing masks or gloves.

- *End-to-End Encryption*: Expanded use of end-to-end encryption for more types of data and communication. For example, end-to-end encryption could be extended to all iCloud data, ensuring that only you have access to your personal information.

5. Integration with Apple's Ecosystem

iOS 19 is likely to further enhance the integration between Apple's various devices and services, creating a more seamless ecosystem experience.

Cross-Platform Features

New cross-platform features could make it easier to switch between and use multiple Apple devices:

- *Universal Control*: The ability to control multiple Apple devices with a single keyboard and mouse, allowing for seamless multitasking. For example, you could move your cursor from your Mac to your iPad and drag files between the two devices effortlessly.

- *Enhanced Handoff*: Improvements to the Handoff feature, allowing you to start a task on one device and seamlessly continue it on another. This might include more types of tasks and better integration with third-party apps.

Cloud and Continuity Features

iOS 19 could introduce new cloud and continuity features to enhance the user experience:

- *Unified File Management*: A more unified approach to file management across devices, making it easier to access and organize your files from any Apple device. This might include a centralized file manager app that syncs your files across iCloud and local storage.

- *Improved Continuity Camera*: Enhancements to the Continuity Camera feature, allowing you to use your iPhone as a webcam for your Mac with higher quality and more customization options.

As we look forward to the release of iOS 19, it's clear that Apple is committed to pushing the boundaries of what its operating system can achieve. From advanced AI integration and augmented reality enhancements to improved user interface and privacy features, iOS 19 promises to be a transformative update. These predictions offer a glimpse into the future of iOS and the exciting possibilities that lie ahead. While we await official announcements and confirmations, the speculation and anticipation surrounding iOS 19 only add to the excitement of what's to come.

Conclusion

The future of iOS is poised to be an exciting frontier, with iOS 18 standing as a monumental leap forward in the evolution of Apple's mobile operating system. This comprehensive update, packed with groundbreaking features and enhancements, sets the stage for even greater advancements in the years to come.

Anticipating the impact of iOS 18 involves understanding how its innovative technologies will reshape user experiences and redefine the capabilities of mobile devices. At the heart of this transformation is the integration of advanced artificial intelligence (AI) and generative AI. These technologies promise to make interactions with devices more intuitive and personalized. Siri, Apple's virtual assistant, will become more conversational and capable of handling complex tasks, thanks to its enhanced language models. This improvement will not only make Siri more efficient but also more contextually aware, providing responses that are tailored to individual users' needs and preferences.

The AI-powered features extend beyond Siri, permeating various built-in apps and system functions. The Messages app, for example, will leverage AI to generate custom emojis and auto-complete sentences, making communication more dynamic and engaging. Similarly, the Photos app will incorporate AI-driven photo editing tools, enabling users to enhance their images with ease. The AI enhancements in iOS 18 are designed to make everyday tasks simpler and more enjoyable, fostering a deeper connection between users and their devices.

Preparing for future innovations involves recognizing the trends and technological shifts that will shape the landscape of mobile computing. One of the most significant trends is the growing emphasis on personalization and customization. iOS 18's customizable Home Screen experience, which allows users to place app icons anywhere on the grid and change app icon colors, is a step in this direction. This level of customization empowers users to tailor their devices to their unique preferences and workflows, enhancing their overall experience.

Another key area of innovation is the integration of augmented reality (AR). As AR technology continues to advance, it will play a more prominent role in iOS updates. The seamless blending of digital content with the real world will open up new possibilities for education, entertainment, and productivity. For instance, AR could revolutionize how we interact with maps, providing immersive navigation experiences that overlay directions and points of interest onto the physical environment. In education, AR could transform learning by bringing subjects to life through interactive, 3D visualizations.

Security and privacy will remain paramount as iOS evolves. Apple's commitment to protecting user data is evident in the on-device processing of AI tasks in iOS 18. By keeping operations local to the device, Apple ensures that personal information remains private and secure. This approach not only enhances user trust but also sets a benchmark for the industry. Future iOS updates will likely build on this foundation, incorporating even more robust security measures to safeguard against emerging threats.

The integration of AI and machine learning (ML) will continue to deepen, making devices smarter and more capable. The future iterations of iOS will likely see even greater advancements in natural language processing (NLP), allowing for more seamless and natural interactions with virtual assistants and other AI-driven features. Additionally, the proliferation of 5G technology will unlock new possibilities for real-time data processing and cloud-based services, further enhancing the capabilities of mobile devices.

Another exciting prospect is the evolution of developer tools and opportunities. The introduction of Swift, Apple's powerful programming language, has already made a significant impact on app development. Future updates to iOS will likely include enhancements to developer tools, making it easier for programmers to create innovative and high-performance applications. This, in turn, will lead to a richer and more diverse app ecosystem, offering users a wide array of options to enhance their device experience.

In the realm of sustainability, Apple's commitment to reducing its carbon footprint and promoting environmental responsibility will continue to influence iOS updates. Future versions of the operating system may include features designed to optimize energy efficiency and support sustainable practices. For instance, improvements in battery management and power consumption could help extend device lifespan and reduce electronic waste. Additionally, iOS updates could incorporate tools that encourage users to adopt eco-friendly behaviors, such as monitoring energy usage and promoting recycling initiatives.

The impact of iOS 18 will be felt across various sectors, including education and business. In classrooms, the integration of advanced technologies will create more engaging and effective learning environments. Teachers will be able to leverage AI-driven tools to personalize instruction and provide real-time feedback, enhancing student outcomes. In the business world, the productivity and automation features in iOS 18 will streamline workflows and boost efficiency, enabling professionals to focus on higher-value tasks.

As we look to the future, the potential of iOS is limitless. The ongoing advancements in AI, AR, security, and customization will continue to redefine what is possible with mobile devices. Each update will build on the foundation laid by previous versions, driving innovation and enhancing the user experience. The journey from iOS 7 to iOS 18 is a testament to Apple's commitment to pushing the boundaries of technology and delivering exceptional value to its users.

In conclusion, iOS 18 represents a pivotal moment in the evolution of Apple's mobile operating system. Its innovative features and enhancements set the stage for a future where mobile devices are more intelligent, personalized, and secure than ever before. As we anticipate the impact of this groundbreaking update and prepare for future innovations, it is clear that the best is yet to come. Apple's relentless pursuit of excellence and innovation will continue to shape the future of mobile computing, creating new possibilities and transforming the way we live, work, and connect. The future of iOS is bright, and the journey ahead promises to be both exciting and transformative.

Appendices

Appendix A: Key Terminology and Concepts

Artificial Intelligence (AI)

Artificial Intelligence (AI) refers to the simulation of human intelligence in machines that are programmed to think and learn like humans. In the context of iOS 18, AI plays a crucial role in enhancing user experience through features like Siri's conversational capabilities and AI-powered photo editing tools. Understanding AI is fundamental as it underpins many of the advanced functionalities in iOS 18, enabling more personalized and efficient interactions with the device.

Generative AI

Generative AI involves algorithms that can create new content, such as text, images, or music, based on input data. In iOS 18, generative AI is used to create custom emojis in Messages and to enhance Siri's ability to generate natural, context-aware responses. This technology significantly expands the creative possibilities for users, making interactions more dynamic and engaging.

Siri

Siri is Apple's virtual assistant, designed to help users perform tasks using voice commands. In iOS 18, Siri has undergone a major overhaul, becoming more conversational and capable of handling complex multi-step tasks. By leveraging advanced language models, Siri now provides more accurate and contextually relevant responses, making it a more indispensable part of daily life.

Spotlight Search

Spotlight Search is a powerful search feature in iOS that allows users to quickly find apps, contacts, emails, and other content on their device. In iOS 18, Spotlight Search has been enhanced with AI to deliver smarter, more relevant search results, improving the overall user experience by making information more accessible.

Augmented Reality (AR)

Augmented Reality (AR) overlays digital information onto the real world, enhancing the user's perception of their environment. iOS 18 integrates AR in various applications, offering immersive experiences that blend digital content with the physical world. This technology opens new possibilities for gaming, education, and productivity on iOS devices.

Home Screen Customization

Home Screen Customization in iOS 18 allows users to personalize their Home Screen by placing app icons and widgets anywhere on the grid, creating custom layouts, and changing app icon colors. This flexibility empowers users to tailor their device's appearance and functionality to their preferences, enhancing usability and aesthetic appeal.

AI-Generated Notifications

AI-Generated Notifications use artificial intelligence to prioritize and manage notifications based on their importance and relevance to the user. This feature helps users stay organized and focused by filtering out less critical notifications and highlighting those that require immediate attention.

Health App Innovations

The Health App in iOS 18 introduces new features such as mental health tracking, sleep analysis, and improved integration with third-party fitness apps. These enhancements provide users with comprehensive tools to monitor and improve their physical and mental well-being, making health management more accessible and effective.

Control Center Redesign

The Control Center in iOS 18 has been redesigned to offer a more streamlined and intuitive interface. It includes updates to the music widget, improved controls for HomeKit accessories, and new accessibility features, making it easier for users to manage their device settings and connected home devices.

RCS (Rich Communication Services)

RCS is an advanced messaging protocol that enables richer communication experiences, such as text effects, suggested replies, and media sharing. In iOS 18, the Messages app supports RCS, enhancing the messaging experience with more interactive and dynamic features.

Appendix B: Frequently Asked Questions

Q: What makes iOS 18 different from previous versions?

A: iOS 18 represents a significant leap forward for Apple's mobile operating system, integrating advanced artificial intelligence and generative AI across various applications. Major updates include a more conversational and capable Siri, AI-powered features in Messages and Photos, and extensive customization options for the Home Screen. These enhancements make iOS 18 the most upgraded version in Apple's history, offering a more personalized, efficient, and engaging user experience.

Q: *How has Siri improved in iOS 18?*

A: Siri has undergone a major overhaul in iOS 18, becoming more conversational and capable of handling complex, multi-step tasks. Powered by advanced language models, Siri can now provide smarter, context-aware responses that take into account a user's history and preferences. Additionally, Siri's on-device processing ensures user data remains private and secure, making it a more indispensable tool for everyday tasks.

Q: *What are the new AI-powered features in iOS 18?*

A: iOS 18 introduces several AI-powered features across different apps and system functions. The Messages app can generate custom emojis and auto-complete sentences based on message content. The Spotlight search feature has been enhanced with AI to surface more relevant information. The Photos app includes AI-powered photo editing tools, making it easier to enhance and personalize images. These AI integrations enhance the overall user experience by providing more intelligent and responsive functionality.

Q: *Can I customize my Home Screen in iOS 18?*

A: Yes, iOS 18 offers extensive Home Screen customization options. Users can place app icons and widgets anywhere on the grid, create blank spaces, and change app icon colors. These features allow for greater personalization, enabling users to tailor their Home Screen layout and appearance to their preferences.

Q: *What are the new features in the Health app?*

A: The Health app in iOS 18 includes several new features aimed at improving users' physical and mental well-being. These features include mental health tracking, sleep analysis, improved integration with third-party fitness apps, new workout modes, and a redesigned Fitness+ interface. These enhancements provide users with comprehensive tools to monitor and improve their health.

Q: How has the Control Center been redesigned in iOS 18?

A: The Control Center in iOS 18 has been redesigned to offer a more streamlined and intuitive interface. Updates include enhancements to the music widget, improved controls for HomeKit accessories, and new accessibility features. These changes make it easier for users to manage their device settings and connected home devices.

Q: What is RCS, and how does it improve messaging in iOS 18?

A: RCS (Rich Communication Services) is an advanced messaging protocol that enables richer communication experiences, such as text effects, suggested replies, and media sharing. In iOS 18, the Messages app supports RCS, enhancing the messaging experience with more interactive and dynamic features, making it easier to communicate in more expressive ways.

Q: What privacy features are included in iOS 18?

A: iOS 18 continues Apple's commitment to user privacy with enhanced privacy and security features. Siri's on-device processing ensures user data remains private and secure. Additionally, AI-generated notifications help prioritize and manage notifications based on their importance, further enhancing user control over their information.

Q: How does iOS 18 integrate augmented reality?

A: iOS 18 integrates augmented reality (AR) in various applications, offering immersive experiences that blend digital content with the physical world. AR in iOS 18 enhances gaming, education, and productivity, providing users with new ways to interact with their environment and digital content.

Q: What developer tools are available in iOS 18?

A: iOS 18 offers new developer tools and opportunities, including enhancements to the Swift programming language. These tools enable developers to create more advanced and efficient applications, taking advantage of the latest technologies and features in iOS 18.